Answering the Bell

Brett Knapp

ANSWERING THE BELL

Answering the Bell
Attn: Brett Knapp
P.O. Box 14121
Minneapolis, MN, 55414

www.mfdbook.com

First printing 2003

ISBN 0-9744103-0-6

LCCN 2003095899

To my family, for its patience
To the MFD, for its excellence

Acknowledgments

This book could not have been written without the inexhaustible cooperation of many people. First, I would like to thank Minneapolis Fire Chief Rocco Forté. By giving me unfettered access to ride along at Station 14 for six months between July and December of 2002 — and knowing that my observations would be published for all to see — Chief Forté displayed a remarkable confidence that his fire department would not be found lacking. Indeed, I was impressed daily by the levels of professionalism and training I witnessed while riding and living with Engine Company 14 and Ladder Company 10 on the A shift. Thanks also go to MFD public information officer Kristi Rollwagen, who provided me with vital details, research, and other information time and again. I would also like to thank each of the captains who allowed me to occupy the empty seat on their rigs on emergency calls — including Tim Baynard, Kris Lemon, Cherie Penn, and Tom Rogalski. Thanks also to the many firefighters who graciously shared their space, time, and stories with me on my days at Station 14, including, but not limited to: Mark Anderson, Troy Bjornstad, Julie Caouette, Leonard Crawford, Al Daher, Steve Drew, Heidi Elmer, Shawn Modahl, Bob Niznik, Laura Pawlacyk, Dan Schultz, Jay Wells, and Elondo Wright. There were several other officers and firefighters with whom I visited at other stations that helped me better understand the details of specific emergency calls and the job in general, including but not limited to: Battalion Chief Donald Leedham, Battalion Chief Jean Kidd, Captain Dana Declouet, Captain Jeff Westall, and firefighter Jackson Millikan. An extra thanks goes out to firefighter Schultz for coming up with the title of the book.

I would also like to thank my editor, Michelle Kibiger, whose keen eye and superior knowledge of language and its usage improved the book immeasurably. You are truly a credit to the craft of writing. I need also to thank the many friends and firefighters who took time to read the book, or portions of it, prior to its being published. Your input made the final product more compelling and more accurate by far. Ditto to Twin Cities fire buff extraordinaire Ron Pearson.

And finally, I wish to express my sincere thanks to the various teachers, friends, family members, writers, and editors who have helped shape my love for reading and good writing over the years.

MFD
2002

Fire Chief
Rocco Forté

Assistant Fire Chief
Ulysses Seal

Cavis Adams
Michael Adams
David Adkins
William Allred
Richard Alm
Timothy Amelse
Dean Anderson
Keith Anderson
Mark Anderson
Robert Anderson
Twanna Anderson
Thomas Arneson
Brian Arradondo

Bilal Atiq
William Aune
Jayson Avent
James Bailey
Frank Baird
Kristen Baird
James Baker
Revonda Baker
Gordon Bates
Paul Baumtrog
Timothy Baynard
Bridget Bender
Randy Berle

Thomas Besch
Paul Besseck
John Bible Jr.
Walter Biesiada Jr.
Brent Bjerkness
Troy Bjornstad
Colm Black
David Blake
Keith Blasingame
Allen Blegen
Bonnie Bleskachek
Kelly Block
Frank Boerboon
Scott Bosell
James Bratton
Brad Brautigam
Harold Breffle
Bradley Bremseth
Jeffrey Brown
Michael Brown
Thomas Brown
Denise Bryn
Charles Brynteson
David Brysky
Timothy Brysky
Anthony Buchanan
Arthur Buckner
Joseph Buffalo
Thomas Burnley
Steven Burns
Scott Campbell
Julie Caouette
Daniel Carlson
Virgil Carlson
Micheal Carswell
Daniel Casper
Jaime Chacon
Roger Champagne
Jonathan Chelstrom
Thierry Chevallier
Richard Christensen
Sean Churchill-Weekes
James Clack
Thomas Clark
Stephen Coffman

Daniel Connolly
Jennifer Cornell
Calvin Covington
Scott Craigie
William Craigie
Leonard Crawford Jr.
Thomas Crowley
Raymond Cruz
Abdul Cunningham
Christopher Daeger
Alec Daher
James Dahl
Michael Dahlberg
Maria Dalton
Keith Daniel
James Dare
Carolyn Davidson
John Davison
Timothy Davison
Dana Declouet
Thomas Deegan
Barry DeLude
David Dewall
Trevor Dewey
John Dick
Michael Dickinson
Jason Dohm
Shana Dooley
John Dorn
Curtis Drew
Steven Drew
Daniel Drews
Norman Drews
Robert Duggan
Stephen Dziedzic
Timothy Dziedzic
Daniel Eason
Steven Ebert
Perry Ebner
Kraig Egeland
Jason Ehmke
Ronald Eickholt
John Eland
Christopher Ellison
Heidi Elmer

Jeffrey Erickson
Steven Erickson
Vicki Erickson
Timothy Evavold
Thomas Fellegy
John Fernandez
Rosita Fields
Jason Firchau
James Fjerstad
Julie Flaskamp
James Flavin
Derrick Foster
John Fruetel
Gerald Fuerstenberg
Ronald Fuller
Michael Fust
Michael Fyle
Thomas Fyle
George Galonska
Allison Garver
Lee Gatlin Jr.
Douglas Gilbert
David Gillen
Jeffrey Goar
Michael Goodwin
Corey Graham
Christopher Gram
Stephen Green
Darrin Gregory
Thomas Griffin
James Hanley
Robert Hanson
Shanna Hanson
Lisa Harding
James Hart
Larry Hartel
Neil Havron
Cory Hermann
Christopher Herrlin
Chad Hess
Mark Hess
Loren Hillesheim
Timothy Hillmeyer
Mark Hilton
Vicki Hoff

Christopher Holloway
Dennis Holman
Bobby Holmes
Charlotte Holt
Douglas Hordyk
Kyle Huggett
John Hupp
Thomas Hupp
Christopher Husnik
Gary Hyatt
Michael Hyska
Ched Ihme
Alex Jackson
Sandy Jackson
Vincent Jackson
Brian Jacobsen
Brent Jacobson
Brent Jagers
Eric Jagers
Mark James
Benard Jangula Jr.
Yin Jiang
Ronald Jogodka
Sourasack Johnnasack
Alan M. Johnson
Alan W. Johnson
Antonette Johnson
Jennifer Johnson
Michael Johnson
Roger Johnson
Stephanie Johnson
Wendy Johnson
Casidy Jones
DaRoss Jones
Karen Jones
Chad Juncker
Rita Juran
Jean Kidd
Maurice King Jr.
Shawn Klancke
Jonathan Klepp
Timothy Klug
John Knoblauch
Brian Kohn
Keith Kohn

Chad Komarec
Wolodymyr Komarec
Debra Koreen
Michael Korogi
Michael Kos
Scott Krepela
Gerald Krueger
Stephen Kubik
Anthony Kuczek
Frank Kurth Jr.
Randolph Kutter
Kenny LaCroix II
Gregory LaFerriere
Jacob LaFerriere
Peter Lage
Mark Lakosky
Stacey Lakosky
Joseph Lane Jr.
Christine Langenberger
Kaci Langums
David Larkin
Bradley Larson
Craig Lasley
Kasimir Lawrynowicz
Walter Lee
Donald Leedham
Kristina Lemon
John Levens
Grant Limke
Jennifer Lindberg
William Lindberg
David Lindfors
Joseph Lompart
Michael Longman
Dennis Mack
Robert Madaras
David Maikke
Peter Malinosky
Mary Maresca
Gregory Martin
Robert Martin
Joseph Mattison
Matthew May
Jacquetta McCabe
Keven McCalister

Carla McClellan
Mark McClun
Anthony McDonald
Susan McKenna
Kalimba McKenzie
Brandon McLaughlin
Roy Meihofer
Carol Melloy
William Merrill
Melanie Metz
Michael Meyer
Cynthia Miller
Joseph Miller
Randall Miller
Tanya Miller
Jackson Millikan
Trevin Mitchell
Shawn Modahl
Mary Mohn
Michael Montgomery
Edward Montiel
Prentice Moore
Tracy Moore
Anne Moss
Colleen Mullen
Kathleen Mullen
Siobhan Mullen
Mark Munson
Stanley Murzyn Jr.
Gerard Murzyn
Daniel Nalepka
Scott Nebel
Eileen Nelson
Eric Nelson
Linda Nelson
Luke Nelson
Paul Nemes
Mark Neu
Teresita Neumann
David Neumiller
David Newell
Matthew Nielsen
Christie Nixon
Robert Niznik
Andrew Norrgard

Jeremy Norton
Troy Nortrom
Henry Ocampo
Larry Oker
Daniel Olson
Mark Olson
Noelle Olson
Robert Olson
Sean Olson
Jeffrey Ostberg
Jacqueline Osterman
Edward Otis
Harlan Ott
Thomas Oxborough
Benjamin Page
Michael Papasodora
Shelly Paulson
Laura Pawlacyk
Travis Payer
Andrew Pederson
Dennis Pekos
Cherie Penn
Michael Pentz
Robert Pentz
Kirk Perez
David Pergande
William Petersen
James Peterson
Russell Peterson
Greg Phillips
Gary Piekarczyk
William Pielow
Elizabeth Pierson
Shari Pierzina
Laura Pilon
Lorin Plante
Stephen Pleasants
Amy Powers
Carrie Preusse
Walten Priest Jr.
Michael Raeker
Warren Raiche
Raul Ramos
Brian Randle
Chad Rathbun

Gaylen Raze
Ladd Ream
Jason Reece
Justin Reid
Ross Repke
Darick Rhodes
Melanie Rich
Grant Riedemann
Dominic Rigert
Drake Ritchie
Curtis Rivers
Jeffrey Rivers
Jason Roberts
Richard Robinson
James Rodger Jr.
James Rodger
Roberto Rodriguez
Thomas Rogalski
Kristin Rollwagen
John Romero
Jerry Rossi
Kevin Rousseau
Donald Rowell III
Charles Rucker
Michael Rumppe
Andre Rush
Chad Saloka
Paul Sam
Joseph San Roman
Maximo San Roman Jr.
Maximo San Roman
Keith Sandberg
Richard Sandusky
Robert Sayers
Roger Schatzlein
Walter Schirmer
Gerald Schmitz
Bradley Schmoll
Amber Schneider
John Schroeder
Dan Schultz
Joe Schulz
Wayne Schuman
Michael Seide
Somsavay Senevisai

Robert Senkyr Jr.
Leonard Senkyr
Toni Serrata
Andre Sewell
Patrick Sexton
Julie Shelstad
Anura Si-Asar
Lee Silbernagle
Joseph Silva
Joel Smith
Sean Smith
David Soderholm
Jennie Soderholm
Steven Solem
Raymond Sombrio
Linda Sone
Steven Sorbel
Gary Spohn
Grant Springer
Leann Stearns
Todd Steinhilber
Laurence Stellenberg
Isadore Stewart
John Stinson
Troy Svenddal
Patrick Swaggert
Staffan Swanson
Marie Swerdfiger
John Szczech
Dylan Taylor
Milagros Taylor
Tracy Terbell
Michael Terry
James Thomas Jr.
Sean Thomas
Sydny Thomas
Timothy Thomas
Helena Thompson
John Thompson
Leonard Thompson
Shane Thorn
Thomas Thornberg
Keith Thorson
Merry Thurn
Frank Thurner

Mark Thurner
Jeffrey Titcomb
Joshua Tjaden
Byron Todd
Robben Todd
Marianna Toth
Daniel Tracy
Michael Tracy
Barry Trebil
Ted Troan
Joshua Tunks
Richard Turner
Bryan Tyner
James Ujke
Wesley Van Vickle
Thomas Villagomez
David Vincent
Anthony Vossen
Sherri Waisanen
Lawrence Wajda Jr.
David Walburg
Jon Walstead
Celester Webb
Edward Weiberg
Jay Wells
Christen Weltin
John Welton
Anthony Wendt
Jeffrey Westall
Gary Westbrook
George Wheeler
Jerry White
Todd White
Thomas Wiley
Anthony Wilson
Reid Wilson
Merrill Wisner
Daniel Wisniak
John Wong
Elondo Wright
Peter Zenk Jr.
Kevin Ziegler
Leslie Ziesemer
Jay Zumberge

Important Terms

• **Apparatus** - Another term for fire engines.

• **Apparatus floor** - Area in firehouse where fire engines are kept.

• **Charged line** - A hose that is filled with water.

• **Cockloft** - The space between a ceiling and the roof or floor above.

• **Coop** - The room in the firehouse where the log book is kept and emergency calls come in.

• **Engine** - The fire rig that carries water, hose, and a pump.

• **Halligan tool** - A steel prying tool, named after its inventor — Huey Halligan, a former firefighter in New York City.

• **Ladder** - The fire rig that carries an aerial ladder, as well as other search-and-rescue and ventilation tools.

• **Line** - Another term for a fire hose.

• **Truckies** - The members of a ladder company.

Foreword
by MFD Fire Chief Rocco Forté

I grew up and went to school near Fire Station 4 in Minneapolis, and I remember watching in awe as the fire engines came screaming out of the big doors of the station and down the street. When I was 12 years old, I also noticed that they would leave the bay doors open at Station 4 when it was warm during the summer. On one such day, I snuck in through the open doors, past the big red rigs, and tiptoed upstairs. Then, although I was very nervous about getting caught, I couldn't resist sliding the tall, silvery fire pole down to the floor below. What a thrill it was. Well, it was a thrill until I turned around and came face to face with a firefighter, who sternly instructed me never to do it again before wishing me a good day.

My next experience with firefighting came after I entered navy boot camp at the age of 17, and I really began to love it. After I got out, I decided to become a teacher, but when I was doing my student-teaching, I realized that I was drawn back to firefighting and applied to the Minneapolis Fire Department. I made it on to the department back in 1975, and have not regretted it once since then.

Firefighting is the perfect job. There is instant gratification that comes with every emergency run you go on because you get to help people right on the spot. I also loved the family atmosphere in the firehouse. It's a great life out there in the fire stations, and readers of this book will see why.

Few jobs help you keep things in perspective in life like firefighting. For me, that perspective came primarily as part of two different incidents while I was riding the rigs. The first was back in the winter of 1983. A fire broke out at 15th and LaSalle, and I was part of the search-and-rescue effort. In a smoke-filled room, I came across a woman and her baby who were trapped. The baby was sleeping in a cardboard box on the floor. I scooped the woman up with one arm and the baby in the other, but each time I tried to stand up to carry them out, the baby began choking on the smoke that was collecting higher up in the room. So I removed my air mask and placed it over the baby's face, then fought my way back outside. By the time I made it, I had inhaled a lot of smoke. It landed me in the hospital for a couple of days, but any firefighter would tell you it's worth the price to save a life. And it also made me realize just how fragile life is, especially when it comes in contact with fire. It made me realize how important it is to cherish every day with your friends and family. That's what matters in life.

The other incident was devastating for me. Two years out of rookie school, a good friend of mine named Grant Benson was killed at the age of twenty-six in a fire in an auto body shop on Lake Street. Arson has since been determined to have been the cause of the fire that killed my friend. It was by far the most difficult thing I have had to deal with on the job. But Grant's death made me a better firefighter, as it forced me to realize that I had to focus on becoming a better firefighter myself. Rather than leaning on what I had already I learned, I dedicated myself to learning, training, and improving myself for the rest of my career. Getting better every day is a goal we want all of the firefighters in Minneapolis to share as we move into the future.

The future will continue to pose new challenges to the firefighters in our city, as we face new threats from possible terrorist attacks, as well as the expected increase in EMS calls as our population grows older. And, of course, we will continue to battle the dangers of fire. In order to adequately protect the citizens of Minneapolis, our department needs to have twenty-seven rigs in service at all times, with each rig carrying four firefighters. This will put us in line with the 1710 standard of the National Fire Protection Association. Currently, we do not meet that standard. And recent budget cuts have set us back a bit further. But as we continue to raise the awareness of the public, the City Council, and the Mayor, I am confident we will meet those national staffing standards someday soon. We have a business plan in place for this. We will get there.

As we continue to strive to get our fire department up to national staffing standards, we will also continue to stay focused on diversity. Our hiring practices in the past several years have helped us become the most diverse big-city fire department in the nation. Outside of the lives and property that have been saved, achieving this diversity is — by far — the biggest achievement of the Minneapolis Fire Department. We will continue in these efforts.

The Minneapolis Fire Department is one of the best-trained, best-equipped fire departments in the country, and I would like to thank the sworn and civilian members of our department for their hard work and dedication to the city.

Rocco Forté
Fire Chief
Minneapolis Fire Department
August 2003

An open letter to the reader:

Some of the firefighters you are about to read about were laid off by the City of Minneapolis in the spring of 2003. The reason for these layoffs was budget cuts (some of which are foreshadowed in the pages of this book) imposed on the department by the city council and the mayor's office. Any government's primary duty is to protect its citizens. Thus, any government that forces its fire or police departments to "do more with less" fails in this most fundamental responsibility. Before any — any! — other entity receives a penny of public tax dollars, your local fire and police departments should be given what they need to operate at full capacity. I hope those who make the funding decisions in Minneapolis will find this book educational.

Brett Knapp
August 2003

ANSWERING THE BELL

Friday night is falling rapidly in Minneapolis, coming down dark and menacing on the city's teetering North Side. The weather outside Fire Station 14 is crisp and comfortable, but a wind is beginning to stir and stiffen, sending violent, rustling shivers through the branches of the massive maple tree that stands sentinel near the station's front doors.

The day has not been an overly strenuous one for the firefighters at Station 14 — a handful of medical calls, a car accident, a stove fire — but the twenty-four-hour shift is but half over. And now that darkness is creeping into the city at the dawn of a new weekend, the firefighters here know to expect anything. Station 14 has been called the "blood and guts" station — "the knife and gun club" is another popular one — by the firefighters who work here. Not only do they hustle to put out fires that feed on this area of the city's aging architectural infrastructure, they also routinely respond to shootings, stabbings, and other violent acts that flare up here — on what often seems like a far too regular basis.

Shortly after ten o'clock the alarm bell rings out, and the seven firefighters on duty tonight rush to the two big fire engines waiting on the cold, gray apparatus floor. The pumper truck, Engine 14, is first out of the station's wooden doors, followed closely by the ladder truck, Ladder 10, and both crash screaming and wailing into the night. They don't have to go far, only one block east and another block to the north. A right turn on to 34th Avenue and the fire reveals itself. Parked squarely next to the curb half a block down is a small white vehicle, its entire rear half engulfed in glowing orange flame. As the fire engines pull closer, the flames dance madly wherever they can find a footing on the vehicle's surface, as if beckoning all comers.

Al Daher, Engine 14's captain tonight, radios to dispatch that they have an auto fire, fully involved, as firefighter Dan Schultz takes the rig in closer, its red flashing lights now lighting up the dark smoke. Daher instructs Schultz to pull all the way past the vehicle on its left and stop a bit further down the street, near the corner hydrant. As Schultz urges the rig past the car, something — a tire, perhaps a window — explodes with a loud bang, and a cloudburst of sizzling orange sparks lunges menacingly toward the fire engine. The firefighters don't even flinch, though, and the sparks cascade harmlessly down the side of the rig as it passes.

Ladder 10 has come to a stop further back down the street, and the fire engines have the flaming vehicle hemmed in on both sides now. As firefighter Laura Pawlacyk, who has slipped from her back seat on Engine 14 and onto the street, dons the last of her protective gear and pulls her oxygen mask over her face, Daher and Schultz pull the first-attack line from the bed of the pumper. The heavy hose flops onto the pavement. The four-person crew of Ladder 10 is walking through the darkened street toward the blazing vehicle, the light from the flames bouncing psychedelically off the reflective striping on their turnout pants, bunker coats, and the polished metal heads of the axes slung menacingly over their shoulders.

Schultz revs up the massive diesel-powered pump on Engine 14 as Daher and Pawlacyk march into the billowing gray smoke with the hose. The line charges and stiffens, drawing its water from the pumper's 500-gallon tank, and Pawlacyk, with Daher right behind her, opens the nozzle on the flaming vehicle, aiming into the driver's side window first. In an explosion of angry noise, the fire hisses and gurgles in protest. It proves to be a stubborn one, and when the gas tank ruptures, spilling a new source of fuel on the pavement beneath the sizzling under-carriage of the vehicle, the flames rise up around and through the vehicle with renewed vigor. Firefighters Shawn Modahl and Troy Bjornstad have been hammering away at the trunk and hood of the vehicle in attempt to get them open, but the gas rupture and the fire's renewed tenacity push them back for the moment.

Tom Rogalski, captain of Ladder 10, realizes this firefight might just require more water than Engine 14 has on board, so he redirects Modahl and Bjornstad to prepare a nearby hydrant. Soon a fresh and limitless supply of water is being routed from the hydrant through Engine 14's pump via a massive yellow hose.

While Pawlacyk and Daher continue to battle the fire with their line, Rogalski and firefighter Mark Anderson begin preparing a foam eductor. After it's attached to the attack line, it will imbue the water with a white slurry to help neutralize the intense brew of vapors and chemicals that continues to renew and feed upon itself underneath the vehicle.

The spectacle has drawn the usual curious crowd of onlookers. One man is sitting — legs crossed, a cigarette dangling from his lips — on a large brick just down the street, watching the firefighters battle the flames as casually as if he were slumped down in front of the television in his own living room.

Soon the foam is ready and being fed onto the flames, and they finally begin to weaken. The ladder crew moves in through the smoke to take another whack at the hood and trunk, and after some hard pounding, both are soon opened. Pawlacyk redirects the stream, and the flames within the engine compartment are drowned in the frothing, white liquid. The fire is finally out some fifteen minutes after the firefighters first began their assault, and Pawlacyk gives the charred shell of the vehicle, which is dripping in on itself like a melting campfire marshmallow, one final bath.

A report comes over the captains' radios that the car was reported stolen earlier in the night. Someone apparently had it in mind to go for a joyride tonight, but didn't want to hassle with a trivial detail like using his or her own vehicle. Once they were through having their fun with the stolen ride, they probably decided to keep the good times rolling by torching it and watching it burn from a distance. Or maybe they just wanted to destroy any incriminating evidence. That will be for the police and the arson investigator to determine, and both arrive and go to work doing just that as the firefighters pack up their hose and tools and roll back to the station.

Some of the firefighters climb the stairs up to the dormitory for bed, while a few find seats in the dining room and amuse each other with card tricks. The inter-department radio speaker squawks continuously as fire companies from around the city are dispatched every few minutes or so. Their sirens can be heard through the speakers as the captains radio in to announce that they are on the move.

It's not quite midnight when another call comes in to Station 14. Someone on Fremont Avenue North called in a shooting, and Engine 14's crew is being summoned — Minneapolis firefighters are trained Emergency Medical Technicians and respond to all 911 calls for medical help — to assist police and paramedics with the victim, or, as is sometimes the case, victims. Shootings are not considered an unusual event at Station 14. The Minneapolis Fire Department responded to more than a hundred shootings in 2001, and the North Side is always home to more than its share of the city's gunplay.

Schultz trots to the rig from the dining room as Pawlacyk and Daher come sliding down the pole. The fire engine pulls out and heads east into the dark night. But Schultz does not take the rig all the way in to the address, as they are making a Code 4 response. They drive with lights and sirens, but Schultz stops a block short of the scene until police radio that they have brought the situation under control.

Engine 14 and the ambulance from North Memorial Medical Center arrive about the same time and stack up a block away. As they wait, a cyclone of police cars whirls in from the surrounding streets, charging toward the area where the shooting took place. A few minutes later, dispatch informs the waiting medical vehicles that police have secured the area and it is safe — safe being a relative term in this line of work — to move in.

Schultz wheels the fire engine up the street, where the flashing lights of a half-dozen police cruisers are controlling the scene in front of a row of small white houses near True Love Church. The firefighters grab their medical bags and ascend the steep, sloping front yard of one of the houses. Like something out of an old gangster movie, the white, jutting beams of police flashlights knife their way between several of the houses as officers search for victims and suspects alike. In the dark between two of the houses, police are tending to a boy who appears to be in his middle to late teens. The firefighters, protective latex gloves strapped into place to protect them from blood and other fluids, move in and take over. The boy is skinny, with baggy jeans slung low around the back of his legs. His right pant leg is soaked with blood from the knee down. He is lying on his back with his arms folded over his face as he rocks back and forth in agony.

Daher begins talking to the boy to keep him alert and get what information he can about the shooting and his injuries as the other firefighters remove the boy's shoes and pull his jeans off. His name is Carl, and in between anguished cries, he begs the firefighters to give him something to ease the pain.

"I feel like I'm gonna throw up and pass out! I'm gonna pass out!" he screams.

"We can't give you anything for that right now," comes Daher's response, "but we're going to get you fixed up as fast as we can, okay?"

"Man, put me out, man," Carl moans over and over.

As Schultz straps an oxygen mask to Carl's face, he quips: "Have my captain tell you a story. That'll put you to sleep." Everyone chuckles, and a grin splits Carl's face beneath the clear plastic mask that is steamed up from his heavy breathing. But despite the smile, the kid remains in pain, and soon he is fighting just to keep his eyes from rolling back into his head as he clings tightly to consciousness. In the dim light, the firefighters can see his dark face has turned an ashen gray.

The firefighters locate a small entry wound on the outside of Carl's calf and an exit wound on the inside, from which a small strip of bloody flesh is dangling. Blood is flowing from the exit wound, and Daher goes to work bandaging the leg as the residents of the houses stand nearby with arms folded tightly to their chests. They wear grim, worried expressions on their faces as they listen to the squawking radios of the police officers who are searching their neighborhood for the shooter, or shooters.

His wounds bandaged, the firefighters lift Carl onto a stretcher and begin retrieving their equipment from the overgrown grass. A quick check with the flashlights shows they've got everything they brought with them. Nothing left behind but a patch of matted, greasy lawn soaked with human blood.

As they move back to the street, the police inform the firefighters they've found another victim lying between two other houses, just two houses down. Another youth, just as thin and just as young as Carl, is sprawled in a tangle of grass and vines and, in an odd similarity, he too has been shot in the leg. Whoever pulled the trigger must not have been shooting to kill.

The second victim does not seem to be in much pain, but as his jeans are tugged off, his sinewy thigh muscles quiver uncontrollably below the hem of his boxer shorts, partially from the chill of the night, but also due, no doubt, to the unnerving situation in which he finds himself. This youth's name is Kevin, and he has been hit in the leg in almost the exact same spot as Carl. But the holes where the bullet entered and exited the calf muscle are just two small red dots and there is little bleeding. The police ask if he knows who shot them.

"We was walking down the street..."

"Who's we?" a cop interjects.

"Me and two friends, we was walking down the street...and these guys...just ran up on us..."

"Do you know who they were, Kevin?"

"Nah, man, we ain't never seen 'em before. One of them had braids...one was wearing a black hood, that's all I seen. My boy said to look out, then they started shooting...and we ran."

A woman who lives in one of the nearby houses steps forward.

"Officer, I think the girl who was with them might be lying back there hurt somewhere," she says, pointing toward the pitch-black alley behind her house. "I saw her run that way."

The police concentrate their search in that area, but find no one else. The girl must have gotten away and is probably huddled somewhere in fear, wondering what to do next, wondering if Carl and Kevin are even alive. Most teenagers don't have to deal with being attacked with guns when walking down the streets of their neighborhood on a Friday night, but those who live on the North Side have to be more wary than most teenagers. She might be watching from a distance, trying to see if her friends are all right but too afraid to come forward in case the shooters are still around. Or maybe she's just running and running, trying to get home, praying she makes it before the sound of gunfire rings out again.

Daher and a paramedic pick Kevin up and carry him down the steps to a stretcher once his leg has been dressed. He is placed in a second ambulance, and Daher goes to the first ambulance to see how Carl is faring.

"Hey, they're going to get you the special treatment," Daher tells him just before the paramedic closes the door, and Carl smiles again and gives the firefighter a thumbs up.

Certain that there are no other victims for them to help, the fire crew takes up and heads back to quarters as the police begin interviewing witnesses and continue searching for evidence. An officer hauls Carl's bloody pants away in a red plastic bag.

Back at the station, the firefighters wipe their arms, forearms, and shoes down with disinfectant wipes, cleansing themselves of the bloody scene. The handheld radio they brought with them will also need cleaning, as it picked up a dark red smear while lying in the grass next to Carl. Once finished, Daher stands on the driveway in front of the station and stares up toward the sky as Pawlacyk heads back upstairs to bed. Schultz settles in to a chair in the dining room and begins flipping around on the television with the remote control. For three people who have just encountered a violent and bloody scene, they are remarkably relaxed and have no trouble settling back into whatever they were doing when the call came in. But then, when you've seen as much blood as these firefighters have seen, you do what you have to, to maintain your own sense of normalcy.

An hour later, Engine 14 is called out again. It's just before two o'clock now, and the pumper zooms to the corner of Penn and Lowry, where a middle-aged woman has crashed her motorcycle. Police and paramedics are already on the scene, and the firefighters move in to lend a helping hand.

The woman is lying flat on her back in the street. She is conscious and does not seem to be in a lot of pain. A car turned recklessly in front of her, she says, and might have grazed the tire of her bike with its bumper, causing her to spill. As the firefighters check her vital signs and apply a neck brace, the paramedics probe her body for pain. She lets out a sharp cry when one of the medics reaches her pelvic area. Soon she's up on the stretcher and on her way to the hospital in the ambulance.

As the firefighters makes their way back to the station, Daher guesses that the woman may have had a broken pelvis and could be in for a long, painful healing process. Then he smiles and adds, "Man, I had just fallen asleep." Pawlacyk chuckles and nods from the back seat. They wonder aloud if they'll be able to get any rest tonight. It's coming up on three in the morning by the time they return, bleary-eyed, and trundle back to bed. Luck smiles on the weary crew, and no more calls come in for the rest of the night. They sleep deeply until just after seven in the morning, shortly before the next shift is set to arrive and take their place.

The firefighters at Station 14 may have only gotten four hours of quality sleep this night, but they'll take it. Four hours is a good night's sleep on a Friday at the "blood and guts" station.

The Minneapolis Fire Department is a young and eager one. Some two hundred firefighters have joined the department over the past three years, and that's out of a total department roster of four hundred and eighty personnel, from the fire chief down to the civilian office staff. The influx is largely the result of a preceding hiring freeze brought on by a lawsuit that choked off annual recruitment for years. All these new firefighters have brought a vibrancy to the department, a chomping-at-the-bit attitude to prove themselves, to soak up all they can about doing the job, and to do that job well. Fire Chief Rocco Forté knows his troops are a bit young, a bit green, right now, but he also believes the city will be set for the long haul once the newer firefighters learn the ropes. But as their confidence burgeons, there will also be a need to avoid a proliferation in the ranks of what one veteran captain calls "Superman Syndrome." That is, the propensity for young firefighters, once they get two or three years of hard-bitten battle with fire under their belt, to feel as if they've mastered the job and begin taking chances. "I'm afraid we might start getting some people hurt," the captain said.

As this new generation of firefighters blossoms, the selfless services they provide will be required more and more by the city of Minneapolis. The fire department here saw its number of responses grow annually almost without exception in the '80s and '90s — from 17,807 total responses in 1982 to 34,802 in 2001. The number of fire calls per year in that time has actually held surprisingly steady, somewhere in the neighborhood of 8,000 to 11,000 annually, although it has been closer to the higher number than the lower for the past decade.

Actual fires, however, are on the decline. As Minneapolis continues to renew itself by building new structures with more effective fire prevention systems and tearing down older and abandoned buildings, the possibility of fire breaking out and causing heavy damage to people and property slowly decreases. There are, of course, new and unprecedented dangers faced by firefighters in an age of skyscrapers and catastrophic terrorist strikes, but for the most part, new technology and improved firefighting techniques have significantly diminished the possibility that large numbers of people will perish in a fire in Minneapolis, as was the case when the three-story Marlborough apartment hotel took nineteen souls with it when it burned to a husk in 1940.

Yet, while it took place more than sixty years ago, the Marlborough fire also serves as a vivid reminder to avoid complacency. Fire is a vicious and underhanded killer, and it always seems to roar back on you just when you think you have it contained, laughing in the face of technology — and the human arrogance that sometimes comes with it. Just one year prior to the Marlborough blaze, the city's fire damage totals were the lowest in twenty-six years. For the first time since 1885, the department had never had to strike anything larger than a two-alarm response. But just three days into the next calendar year, fire dealt the city a grisly death-toll record that still stands six decades later.

Station 14 was built on the city's North Side about that time at the northwest corner of James Avenue and 33rd Avenue North in 1939. The station, with its birth year carved subtly into a massive tan brick near the apparatus doors, was one of three funded largely by President Franklin D. Roosevelt's Public Works Administration, and it became the new home for Engine 14 in 1940, which moved from its fifty-two-year-old digs at 21st Avenue North and Fourth Street, which is just off Broadway, near where it intersects with Washington Avenue. The new Station 14 also welcomed Ladder 10 within its new whitewashed double doors that same year, and the companies have responded side by side to all matter of emergencies ever since.

Perhaps no station in the city has witnessed a bigger shift in the demographics it serves than Station 14. When it first went into service, the neighborhoods of North Minneapolis in its response area were settled predominantly by Jewish families, with enclaves of Irish, German, and Polish immigrants also present. But, as was the case in so many other big cities around the nation at the time, a large chunk of the city's population drained into the suburbs in the '50s, '60s, and '70s, taking with it much of the area's wealth. Despite efforts, many of them relatively successful, to reinvigorate the inner core of Minneapolis, these communities became home to the city's poorest, and increasingly restless, inhabitants. And with the construction of freeways that resulted in the bulldozing of thousands of structures, city-dwellers found their living areas suddenly and strangely mutated, as well as more and more densely packed. Projects sprang up.

With its racially diverse population, the North Side became a tinderbox during the civil rights and anti-establishment disturbances of the '60s, and Station 14 found itself in the eye of the firestorm. All over the nation, fire departments were seen as part and parcel to the white-dominated civic structures that were suddenly absorbing the brunt of Vietnam-era, anti-government wrath. It happened that the vast majority of the nation's firefighters were white men, and despite the selfless and dangerous acts they performed for their communities, their connection with the government and the color of their skin were reasons enough for some people to associate them with the bogeymen of the day — white, male politicians. But government officials didn't have to venture into the city's rougher neighborhoods. Firefighters did, so the citizens lashed out at them instead.

Firefighters in many big cities suddenly found themselves in danger of being harmed by the very citizens they were always rushing to protect. Rocks, bricks, and other objects were hurled at fire engines as they raced to fire scenes. Firefighters clinging to the sides and rear of fire engines were fully exposed and vulnerable to this flying debris, and it was not uncommon for them to be knocked from their fast-moving rigs, often resulting in serious injury or even death. Many big cities found themselves scrambling to outfit the open-air cabs of their fire engines with makeshift plywood or metal shells that could help protect their firefighters.

Fire engines were not the only target of angrily hurled projectiles, of course. Stationary objects such as structures housing local businesses often proved to be much easier game. In July of 1967, the city's annual Aquatennial festival devolved from a celebration of the city's watery heritage to a desperate dance with a far more malevolent member of the proverbial four elements when someone firebombed a bar on Plymouth Avenue North shortly after ten at night on July 20. Arson and rioting erupted. Soon the city's fire department was scrambling to battle blazes up and down Plymouth, as well as on the south and east sides of the city. A massive lumberyard blaze on the South Side climbed all the way to four alarms shortly after midnight, requiring a huge expenditure of manpower and equipment.

It was about that time when things got really crazy on the North Side.

The rioting was relentless, and a string of businesses was set ablaze. The rioters were feverish, and growing more so as their shadows stretched longer and longer onto the streets under the hellish illumination of the glowing flames. They were determined that these buildings fall to ash, and firefighters arriving on the scene were beaten back by the crowd. It was "burn, baby, burn" on the North Side that night.

Not until some fifty police offers provided a pocket of law and order around the buildings could the firefighters return and get to work on the by-now fully involved structures. One of the buildings was so completely engulfed as to require a second alarm. Before the night was over, nearly every off-duty firefighter had been called into action, as were several fire companies from St. Paul. But while the flames were knocked out in a matter of hours, the emotional coals that sparked the conflagration in the first place still glowed hot in certain parts of the city.

Today the North Side of Minneapolis is essentially hemmed in on three sides by highways — Highway 55 and Interstates 94 and 694 — with Xerxes Avenue providing the fourth border on the west. A good portion of the metro area's middle and upper classes zoom in and out of downtown to work each day on the highways that enclose this northernmost hunk of the inner city. Although they pass so closely to it every day, the commuters simply go round and round the North Side without ever desiring, or daring, to enter this part of the city. The North Side is now home to a poorer class of families, many of them black and, increasingly, Asian and Hispanic.

But while the civil rights struggle of the '60s and '70s has settled into the history books, there is another struggle that goes on daily on the North Side, a never-ending tug-of-war between poverty and prosperity, modest though that prosperity might be. Throughout the neighborhoods on this side of the city, particularly the older sections south of Lowry Avenue, blocks and blocks of aging residential areas are the battlegrounds. Nearly every house here is decades old, and many are falling into disrepair or being abandoned as the families who live here struggle to pay the bills each month. Oftentimes they can't make ends meet, and so another house is boarded up to await an unknown fate, while the family that lived there is forced to find shelter elsewhere, perhaps crammed in with friends or relatives who have barely enough space for themselves. Many yards are overgrown to the point that houses look as if they're sinking slowly into the earth. Others have little vegetation at all and are littered with trash and decaying household furniture.

The abandoned houses are often broken into by homeless folks, or drug dealers and prostitutes. Some scrape their way desperately through the plywood covering the doors or windows to find shelter from a wickedly harsh winter's night, while others turn them into dens of crime and sleaze. Many times they catch fire, or are set on fire, while illegally occupied, and it is the fire department's job to not only extinguish the fires, but to make weekly sweeps through the neighborhoods to make sure the plywood barriers on these abandoned houses have not been breached.

While these empty houses account for a good percentage of Station 14's fire runs, the fire department responds far more often to the houses where people live legally but poorly. Though there are often more people living in many of these houses than can be comfortably or sanitarily accommodated, many have no other choice. Children suffer neglect and other forms of abuse. The struggle to merely subsist is an ongoing one, and many families depend on welfare benefits to get by. The firefighters at Station 14 know to expect an increase in heavy-trauma medical runs toward the end of each month. Stabbings, shootings, beatings, and domestic abuse calls all seem to be more prevalent in the waning days of the month. That's when the latest welfare handouts or meager paychecks begin drying up, and people begin to fight over the last of the money.

"It's survival," says firefighter Julie Caouette. "People do more extreme things to get their means. People can go get a job at Burger King and work their way up there, I guess, but other things must just seem so out of reach. And it just starts becoming survival of the fittest and people start losing perspective of ethics and not realizing that other people are going to pay for it if you steal from a store. It's sad, because people will generalize all these stereotypes towards blacks, but it's not because they're black, it's because they're poor."

But amidst the day-to-day struggle to survive, many residents in the rougher parts of the North Side are making a go of it. For every disintegrating house, there is another that is home to hard-working people who hope for a better life for their families, and they go about trying to build it as best they can. Neighborhood watch groups attempt to put grassroots clamps on crime. At times of the year when the weather is conducive to it, you can see people tidying up their small yards, hauling away trash and adding fresh coats of paint, or making other renovations to their homes — all while houses on either side of them sit vacant and neglected.

The further north you move in this part of the city, the better things get. The houses are younger and, for the most part, well kept by solidly entrenched blue-collar, middle-class families. The streets are newer, wider, and laid out in a standard grid format, unlike some of the narrower and more tangled avenues a bit further south, which can cause headaches for firefighters as they try to navigate them in their massive rigs at high speeds. It is a problem that becomes particularly acute when winter arrives and slopes of freshly plowed snow make for an even tighter squeeze. And while there is plenty of greenery around in the northernmost areas of the North Side, trees in the yards do not grow as rampantly as they do closer to the inner city, where they go untended for years and seem to be crawling the very walls of the houses around them.

Still, there is a strong sense of community on the North Side, and people are more apt to know the people who reside around them. The communal bonds in some neighborhoods here are among the tightest in the metro, especially in comparison to some of the more affluent suburban areas that are little more than vast seas of four-bedroom, three-car-garage islands unto themselves.

And racial tension is not nearly the rampant volcano it was in the '60s, but it is still there and can easily be drawn to the surface under the right circumstances, even in certain instances involving the fire department. For the most part, though, firefighters are well-respected by the residents in this part of the city these days, and the fact that several of the firefighters who work the North Side are black themselves only helps nurture the locals' reverence for them and the service they provide.

But there are times when all-white fire crews responding to a heavily involved house fire in one of the city's more desperate neighborhoods must weather verbal attacks from folks who feel the firefighters aren't doing all they can do to put the fire out. If a house or building is showing a great deal of flame when the fire department arrives on the scene, firefighters are trained to fully ascertain the situation before making their attack. Rarely do they simply leap from the fire engine and charge into a blazing building with hoses gushing. And some people, especially those whose senses are frayed and overwrought by the situation at hand, begin to draw illogical conclusions from the firefighters' calm, deliberate demeanor. In such cases on the North Side, bystanders on occasion accuse white firefighters of allowing their possessions to burn only because they are black.

But the racial blade cuts both ways. Black firefighters in Minneapolis sometimes have to deal with the occasional sideways glance or other attitudes of wariness when arriving on the scene for medical calls in a white household.

"Some (white) people we go to help, you can tell they're jumpy," says firefighter Elondo Wright. "Some patients that we have, it seems like they don't want me to help them because I'm black. There are others where it's very obvious that they don't want you to help them. You sometimes feel like, if you don't want us to help you, whatever, we'll leave. But at the same time, you don't want to feed into what they want you to feed into."

While this country's bout with racism grows more tiresome with each small intolerance, there is reason to take heart. As firefighters can attest, people's racially marred perceptions of others ultimately come back into a much more clear focus at their terminal moment. The humanity they share with people of different skin tones, it seems, becomes most apparent at their moment of greatest vulnerability.

"One thing about people," Wright says, "if they think they're dying, they don't seem to care what color you are."

ANSWERING THE BELL

Firefighters spend a lot of time waiting. Waiting for someone else's personal crisis to touch off a chain of events that will result in ringing firehouse bells and firefighters rushing out to help. And they will go, quickly, flying into the streets with sirens wailing and lights spinning. To help perfect strangers. It is quite a spectacle when they move, something to set the heart racing.

But in between instances of saving the day, firefighters wait. That is not to say that they are idle, which is something very different than waiting. Firefighters bristle at the perception that they merely lounge around and play cards all day while waiting for the next alarm. Much of their "down time" is spent training, reviewing procedures, and keeping their equipment in a state of readiness. Yet, while making every effort to keep themselves honed, they also rest and relax. Inside the two-story brick walls of Station 14, they pass the time in between emergency calls and training periods by talking, laughing, playing dominos, surfing the Internet, watching TV, reading, lifting weights, whatever. Basically living life as normally as anyone who has a few leisure hours to wile away at their own home would. The difference being, the guy at home on his recliner likely won't have to run out to save someone's life with just a moment's notice. Yes, as casual as firefighters make it all look, the nerve-endings just beneath their skin hum, perpetually and keenly. Because they know at any moment those bells can ring, yanking them away from whatever they're doing and sending them catapulting into the city streets to do the work they love to do.

Indeed, every moment of each twenty-four-hour shift is pregnant. The bells can toll at any time and relieve the quiet tension, releasing into the firefighters' veins that familiar gush of adrenaline. If your heart doesn't jump when the bell goes off, one firefighter says, you're in the wrong line of work. A lot of firefighters are, or become, adrenaline junkies. They always know that next call is coming. It is inevitable, so every tick of the clock increases the odds that their anticipation, however subdued, will burst the very next second. Or the next. Or the next.

The weather outside today is sunny and crisp. The station's two fire rigs sit with their noses pressed up against the big wooden doors that open to the outside world, and what an outside world it is, flammable and fraught with hazardous pitfalls just waiting for an unsuspecting human or an unsympathetic spark to come along. Engine 14 carries hose, 500 gallons of water, a few lengths of ground ladder, and a massive pump for drawing water from hydrants to the fire scenes. The crew's primary function on a fire scene is to attack the flames. Ladder — or truck — crews perform search and rescue and help ventilate fire scenes by chopping through doors, busting out windows, and cutting holes in the roof to allow heat, smoke, and volatile gases to escape. Spectators at fire scenes are often shocked to see truckies casually breaking out windows with their axes and other tools, but if they didn't get the heat out, it would be too much for the firefighters inside the structure to handle. Opening things up and letting the smoke out can often make or break efforts to take a fire by the throat. Less smoke means visibility, and if you have visibility, the battle is all but won. Ladder trucks are also often employed to get firefighters up to the roof or windows to perform rescues, or to unleash a gush of additional waterpower from above at larger fires. If engines are the quick-moving, first-strike units, the ladders are the heavy artillery.

All around the apparatus floor, big, empty, rubber boots with fire-resistant bunker pants and red suspender straps curled down around the ankles are sitting near the doors of the fire engines. It's a strange sight — as if whoever was wearing the boots has vanished into thin air, leaving only their garments behind where their human occupants last stood. The boots are placed just so, of course, to give the firefighters an added measure of efficiency when a call comes in. It's all about maximum preparedness. This way they can simply move to the garage, step out of their shoes and into their boots, then up onto the blocky chrome steps of their rigs, all in one smooth succession.

The garage in every fire station smells the same, a faint intermingling of tire rubber, various oils, and diesel exhaust. When you walk past the open doors of the fire rigs, you can also catch a whiff of charred wood. It is a smell that would remind most people of an open fireplace or a recently snuffed campfire. It's sticky stuff, and it clings to — and seems even to become one with — the coats, pants, gloves, helmets, and other gear the firefighters store in the cabs of their rigs.

At the rear of the apparatus floor, firefighter Julie Caouette is sitting on a sturdy, wooden workbench, clad in her dark navy blue uniform shirt and pants, waving her black uniform shoes gently back and forth as they dangle a foot or so above the floor. Sitting near her are firefighters Shawn Modahl and Mark Anderson, the latter of whom has his feet propped up on a shop vac. Together, along with Captain Tom Rogalski, who is upstairs doing paperwork in his office, they make up Ladder Company 10. The last names of all four firefighters — as well as those of Engine Company 14 — have been scrawled in white on an old, green duty chalkboard that hangs on a nearby wall. They began a new shift about two hours ago, and the ladder crew has spent much of its time since then scrubbing the kitchen and dining room spotless. The crew of Engine 14 that shares the "A" shift with them two full days out of every six also expended its share of elbow grease.

They are all relaxing a bit now, pacing themselves as they settle in for another long day ahead. Caouette is regaling her two counterparts with stories about her softball team's recent trip to Seattle, where her club took ninth place out of thirty-eight teams from around the country. One of her teammates is a school teacher in the local suburb of Chaska, and Caouette has suggested to her that some of the firefighters could come speak at her school on one of their off days. The teacher jumped all over the offer, so Caouette is floating the idea to Anderson and Modahl.

Anderson and Modahl are two of the most powerful men on the A shift, and Anderson is easily the most physically imposing. He stands nearly six-and-a-half feet tall and is so hulking that he almost seems to have been constructed out of the torso and limbs of several other massive men. His wide shoulders taper upward past a muscular neck that supports a head that looks almost too small for his huge body. As an 11-year veteran of the department, he is second only to Rogalski in seniority on the A shift at Station 14. Although Anderson is in very good shape, one of his former captains was always amazed at how fast he blew through tanks of oxygen at fires ("All that muscle," the captain observed). Anderson's blond hair is cropped tight to his skull, and he wears large, round eyeglasses atop a long nose that gives him a mild-mannered, bookish appearance. He is also the station's resident character. One minute you'll find him upstairs quietly poring over some dusty tome like *Beowulf* or *Morte d'Arthur* for the umpteenth time, the next down in the TV room bellowing at cartoons or running aloud his own commentary on an old black-and-white movie. His sense of humor tends toward the bawdy and the slapstick, but he is perhaps the most polite and friendly firefighter on the shift when it comes time for that.

Modahl is shorter, stockier, and more soft-spoken than Anderson, but he is also thickly built from head to toe. His arms are short and powerful — too bulky to allow him to reach down and touch his own shoulders when his upper arms are extended straight out from his sides. His cohorts tease that he'd never be able to call a 20-second timeout in basketball because he can't complete the necessary hand-and-arm motion. Modahl's short blonde hair and stolid facial features give him an almost passive appearance. He doesn't make a lot of noise around the station, but he has a reputation around the department as a powerful, hard worker on the fire scene.

"So, how old are they?" Modahl asks.

"Sixth-graders, I think," Caouette replies.

"Sixth-graders?" Anderson booms. "God, they'll kill us. They'll be poking us and kicking us. Kids that age are a nightmare!"

Caouette knows Anderson is only making his usual fun, so she brushes it off with a laugh and continues with her plan.

"I could talk to them a little bit, then shut off the lights and you two could come crawling in like you're doing a search, grabbing their feet and stuff. Then we could have Dan come in through the window."

"We should have Mark come busting through the door with an axe and stick his head in and say, 'Daddy's home!'" Modahl says, and they all laugh some more.

"I could squirt 'em with the pump can," Anderson says, then tilts his head back and lets out one of his trademark, deep-chested, double-shot laughs that can always be heard in the next room.

"huh-HA!"

But all joking aside, and firefighters will joke about just about everything, both Anderson and Modahl agree to give up some of their own free time to drive the forty-five minutes one way to Chaska and put a show on for the kids.

"I'll stand there in the gear, but you do all the talking," Anderson says to Caouette, and she beams at their approval of her plan.

"They'll love it," she says.

"Yeah, I'll come," Anderson says.

"I'll do it if I can make it work," Modahl says, nodding agreeably.

No one speaks for a moment, then Anderson breaks the silence.

"I can't wait to squirt those kids."

Moments later they are joined by Peg Lamb, a thin rail of a woman who looks something like a well-aged movie star from the silent era. Though her body is considerably more frail than it once was, she has not lost an ounce of spunk at the passing of the years. She has lived next to this fire station for thirty years — she brags that she even has more seniority than Chief Forté — and has seen hundreds of firefighters come and go at Station 14. She makes at least one appearance most days, coming in early with her own mug to share a cup of firehouse coffee and chat with the firefighters who always refer to her as "Mrs. Lamb" or "Mom" or "Momma Lamma." Having drawn a cup of coffee in the kitchen, she walks over to where Caouette, Anderson, and Modahl are sitting, and they pull up a chair for her.

Anderson and Mrs. Lamb begin verbally poking at each other; Anderson teasing her for the unusual vest she is wearing over her turtleneck; Mrs. Lamb needling Anderson for not being featured in the local firefighter calendars that are being sold by a local pop radio station to help raise funds for new and expensive thermal imaging equipment. Anderson lets out another booming guffaw, so loud that it startles Mrs. Lamb as she takes a sip of coffee. But she recovers quickly and informs the others that she's been selling the calendars, which feature photos of some of the male members of the department, at a local church.

"Everyone who's bought one has been an old woman," Mrs. Lamb says. "They're all eighty-plus. The pastor's mother bought one and said, 'Oh, I'm going to hang this up right by my bed.' Well, the pastor stepped in and said, 'Oh, I don't know about that.'"

Mrs. Lamb is always happy to do whatever she can to show her support for the department, and the firefighters at Station 14 are glad to reciprocate.

"I had a lot of church raffle tickets to sell one time and these guys bought me out," she recalls. "They put me over the top."

In through the open garage doors walk two paramedics. They are new on this side of town, and they just wanted to stop by and introduce themselves to the local firefighters. After a few minutes of light-hearted banter, several of the firefighters invite the new paramedics to join them in a game of coin toss. In this favored firehouse contest, everyone tosses a coin toward a line on the apparatus floor. The person who comes closest to the line picks up his or her coin and exits the game, leaving the others to toss again. The last person standing has to buy everyone a soda. After a couple of minutes of this, one of the paramedics finds himself digging in his pockets for coins for the pop machine. Freshly-won sodas in hand, the firefighters wave goodbye to their new partners-in-arms.

A few minutes later, at ten-forty in the morning, the waiting ends. An old-fashioned bell, like the ones that still call children in from school playgrounds at recess time, hangs outside on the western wall of the station. It rings first, its brash trilling the first signal that, somewhere nearby, someone needs the fire department's help. Everyone instantly stops talking and stands to move to the rigs. Rogalski appears from the ceiling above as he slides down the pole to the garage. There is always a short pause between the bell and the succeeding electronic pulses that blare through every room in the station. A shorter pause usually signals a medical run, while a longer pause is often a dead giveaway for a fire.

This pause is a long one.

"This is for all of us," Modahl says.

A moment later, the amplified pulsing begins, a handful of steady monotone notes — BEEP BEEP BEEP BEEP BEEP — that confirms that it is indeed a fire. Had it been a medical call, the initial bell would have been followed by up-and-down tones — BEEP beep BEEP beep BEEP beep — and only Engine 14 would respond. But this will be a fire run, and Ladder 10's firefighting prowess will be required.

A woman's disembodied voice blasts over the loudspeakers from downtown's central dispatch.

"Engine 4, Engine 2, Engine 14, Ladder 4, Ladder 10, Rescue 1, Chief 4, a building fire. 1803 Bryant Avenue North. Box 404 Bravo."

The dispatcher repeats the sequence. The box number she gives corresponds to a small section on the fire district map and will help guide the responding companies. Most of the time, a single engine, or as many as two engines and one ladder, make up the first response to a fire call. But the dispatcher is calling for three engine companies and two ladder companies, plus the heavy rescue company and the on-duty battalion chief. This is a full first-alarm assignment, which is struck when the dispatcher has reason to believe that the fire is a substantial one and may be spreading quickly. Occasionally the dispatcher will have a few additional details for the responding units, but the fire department won't know for sure what they are facing until they arrive on scene.

Firefighter Jay Wells jumps into the driver's seat of Engine 14. He ignites the diesel engine and taps the on-board computer to let dispatch know they are en route. A thick bar of red lights on top of the cab flares to life, painting the inside of the garage with electric crimson strokes. Captain Tim Baynard and Dan Schultz have pulled on boots, pants, and coats and climbed into their seats on the rig — Baynard in the passenger's seat and Schultz directly behind Wells. The doors in front of the engine swing open, and Wells feeds the big diesel engine with his foot. It growls back as it rolls out into the clear summer air. The quiet of this modest residential area is torn as Wells hits the sirens and spurs the engine south onto James.

Anderson has the ladder truck rumbling in its berth to the right of where Engine 14 stood. The long extension cords that keep Engine 14's six batteries at full power dangle slowly back and forth from the ceiling. The ladder's doors remain closed until Caouette is in place in the till — a small, enclosed structure perched on the rear of the aerial apparatus where she will control the fifty-seven-foot rig's rearmost wheels. This job requires skill and concentration, or the tail end of the rig is liable to go out of control. On the bulletin board in the station's dining room is a photo of a blue pickup truck, its entire left side crumpled when a rookie firefighter recently lost control in the till. The pickup proved to be no match for Ladder 10, which smashed into it just as it was swinging out of the station.

Rogalski is riding shotgun on the ladder truck, with Modahl now in his seat directly behind him. Caouette taps an electric signal from her spot in the till, which opens the bay doors and lets Anderson know she is ready to go. The long, red dreadnought with gold piping slides into the sunlight and falls in behind Engine 14, which has already made its way to Lowry and headed east.

Wells is pushing the engine hard through the rapidly parting traffic. Over the screaming sirens, the crew hears the squawk of radio reports that Engine 4 has arrived on scene, followed shortly by identical transmissions from Engine 2 and Ladder 4. Engine 14 will be the third arriving — or third-in — engine and will set up as the rapid intervention team — or RIT — in front of the burning structure, prepared to go in if, and only if, fellow firefighters go down and are in need of rescuing. The ladder companies will be in charge of seeking out and rescuing any civilians.

As Wells brings the engine to a stop near the southwest corner of Bryant and 18th, Ladder 4 has already entered the building to begin its searches. A crowd of about two dozen people has gathered and is watching from the southeast corner of the intersection, the glassy blue spine of the Minneapolis skyline gleaming in the distance behind them. Ladder 10 pulls into position, followed by Rescue 1. In all, a half-dozen massive fire rigs and their crews are now strategically positioned around the afflicted structure, a two-story, brick building on the small campus of Church of the Ascension, a Catholic church with a long history on the North Side. A heavy stench of what smells like burning hair fouls the air, and black smoke is slowly spilling from an upper room on the back side of the building, which was built in 1948 and has the look of an old monastery.

Radio loudspeakers on Engine 4 are turned up to a high volume, and the calls going across the radio as the firefighters inside communicate in shouting tones add an element of chaos to the scene. But the firefighters are moving confidently about and doing their work in assigned teams.

Caouette and Anderson slide a 40-foot hand ladder off their truck and set it up at the base of the building, below where the smoke is showing. At the front of the building, three members of Engine 4's crew have pulled a length of two-and-a-half-inch hose off the hose bed and are sprinting up the steps toward the front door, the hose dropping and unfolding behind them as they go. Engine 4's driver, Chris Herrlin, is getting the pump up and running.

Caouette and Anderson are up the ladder now and standing on a landing just outside the smoking window. Modahl and Rogalski have pulled on air masks and joined the search for civilians inside on the first floor, where they encounter light smoke but find no one in need of rescue. Baynard, Schultz, and Wells are fully suited, with air tanks for their self-contained breathing apparatus strapped to their backs. They stand just at the base of the front steps, ready to intervene the moment a fellow firefighter is determined to be in trouble. Hopefully, this will be a boring run for them.

Engine 4 and the other crews inside are all right for now as they fight their way through hallways filled with thick black smoke while trying to find the seat of the fire. They move from door to door, kicking in those that are locked. After about five or six doors, they find the room where the fire has started. Engine 4 can see the orange flames glowing through the smoke.

Outside the building, Caouette and Anderson begin breaking windows to vent the smoke. The firefighters on the other side of an external door are having trouble getting it opened, so Anderson and Caouette take turns whacking at the outer screws holding the door shut with their heavy axes. Soon the door is open, and more black smoke rushes out to fill the fresh air with an acrid stain.

Inside, the fire is burning wildly on a bed, but has not, amazingly, spread much further as of yet. Engine 4's crew quickly knocks it down, and one of the firefighters pulls what's left of the charred, smoking, dripping mattress down the steps and out onto the sidewalk, dumps it there, and heads back inside. A local television crew's camera man, who has been moving around looking for good shots, sees this and rushes over to set up outside the door through which the mattress was ejected.

But there's not much more action to be had at the door, so the camera man joins his reporter in the street, where they set up for a quick interview with Battalion Chief Richard Christensen, who quickly and pleasantly explains that it appears that it was just a mattress fire. There was a lot of smoke, so it looked worse than it was, he says, and no one was hurt, which is good news. The news crew quickly folds up and moves on, probably a little disappointed that the small fleet of visually impressive fire engines and controlled chaos surrounding them did not portend a larger, sexier story they could dramatically broadcast to the masses at 5, 6, and 10. Just a simple mattress fire, but the Minneapolis Fire Department did its job well by responding quickly and en masse to overwhelm it before the flames flooded the old building and did indeed become newsworthy.

The flames now out, the serious expressions on the twenty-some firefighters on the scene melt away and they chat amiably and laugh with each other as they move about, replacing equipment on their rigs. Wells and Baynard help Engine 4 reload its hose, while Caouette, Modahl, and Anderson refit their truck with its ladders, axes, and hooks — the long poles with hooked ends used for pulling down ceilings and walls in search of fire. Schultz stows the RIT gear. Bottled water and sports drinks are distributed to the heated firefighters, who guzzle away.

Engine 14 and Ladder 10 are given permission to take up, and are back to the station by eleven-thirty. A sheet of gray clouds has moved in and blotted the sun from view, and a chilly breeze rushes in sporadically through the open garage doors, causing the wind chime made of glass Dalmatians and fire helmets to jingle nervously.

Schultz and Wells settle in to a pair of chairs on either side of the dining room table and begin watching football highlights on the large TV atop one of the two refrigerators in the room. On the walls, which are painted dark brown and white, hang maps of Minnesota, the United States, and the world, along with a bulletin board that contains official postings, and another that is covered with photographs of fire scenes and moments of levity among the station's firefighters. On the wall opposite the TV is a small shelf bearing an ancient, dusty stereo receiver that is neither plugged in nor connected to anything else. The only purpose it has in life these days is to act as a display perch for a yellowish, waxy piranha that stands frozen in time after a trip to the taxidermy shop.

Wells has been on the department for close to nine years. He's an efficient, aggressive driver with a reputation for delivering his crew to any scene in minimal time, and he knows the pump and inner workings of Engine 14 intimately. Born and raised on the North Side, Wells is a devoted sports fan, particularly when it comes to inner city youth and their exploits on the basketball court. He has a muscular face, and his intense personality has as much effect on the mood of the station as anyone's. A boxing aficionado, Wells keeps himself in good shape, and on one of his burly biceps the words "Persistence Over Resistance" have been tattooed in dark ink around the head of a roaring wild cat.

Sitting next to Wells, Schultz is sipping Diet Coke from a coffee mug. Schultz could be considered the unsung hero of this crew. He approaches his work on any emergency scene with composure and no-nonsense workmanship that helps his entire crew excel. Schultz strives to improve on his skills whenever he can, whether by asking questions of other firefighters or reading up on techniques and strategies. Once a job is completed, he does not seek acclaim in any form, but his observant nature makes him aware of which of his fellow firefighters are doing a good job, and he is always impressed when he notices those who have clearly worked to keep their skills honed. Like many firefighters, he has extra compassion for children and the elderly who get caught up in emergency situations, and he is quick to supply a frightened youngster with a stuffed animal out of the stash that is often kept on the rigs for just such occasions. He also enjoys working to keep the station and the fire engines clean and in good repair. The citizens of the city pay a lot of money for this equipment, he reasons clearly, so it's only right that it be well cared for. In dealing with his station mates, he realizes the value of a good listener and will sit patiently, his hawkish eyes locked in, while a fellow firefighter vents a small grievance or takes him into their confidence over a private matter. And while he can sit through entire conversations impassively to the point of seeming humorless, he is possessed of a self-deprecating dry wit that can make people break out in head-shaking fits of laughter.

Schultz, Wells, and the others have not been resettled in for long when the bell rings again just after noon, this time for a car fire on Interstate 94. Ladder 10 and Engine 14 are both en route and are about to make a turn on to Dowling Avenue, which will provide them the quickest freeway access, when Ladder 4 radios in that they are near the scene and can handle it. The screaming sirens and lights of Station 14's rigs subside instantly, and their speeds drop to normal traffic levels as the firefighters unbutton coats, remove helmets, and relax back into their seats.

After a quick stop at the station, the rigs go their separate ways to pick up food for lunch. For Engine 14, it will be a stop at Kowalski's Market and Subway before returning to quarters. But before they do that, Wells, Baynard, and Schultz set out to familiarize themselves with some of the trickier streets in the area. Schultz is giving thought to taking the test to become a driver sometime in the future, so as they climb into the rig to move out, Wells allows Schultz to take the driver's seat to get some practice behind the wheel.

"Let's go to 14th and Hall Curve," Wells states as he buckles into one of the backseats.

Schultz thinks for a moment about which route would be quickest.

"Lyndale Avenue?" he asks, seeking confirmation.

"Here I am a rookie," Wells quips from the back, "just out of rookie school, and you're asking me."

Wells knows it's important for the department's drivers to be confident when making their own decisions on how to most efficiently arrive at the correct address, and he's letting Schultz know the rig is in his hands, and his hands alone. Schultz thinks for another moment, then checks the map and confirms his hunch.

"Yep, Lyndale to 14th," he says. Schultz can not see it, but Wells is nodding in affirmation as he spurs the fire engine slowly out through the doors and into the street. Wells offers Schultz more advice on the best way to get to certain addresses as they pass through some of the North Side's trickier neighborhoods. Some have dead-ends, one-way streets, or other time-consuming pitfalls that can ensnare unsuspecting drivers, and Schultz absorbs all of Wells' advice with a series of nods.

While they are in the area, the firefighters head west to the small campus of an inner-city community service organization called The City, Inc. Wells wants to hand-deliver an invitation to the black firefighters ball to Spike Moss, The City, Inc.'s vice president. Moss is not in today, but the women at the front desk assure Wells that he will get the invitation if he leaves it with them, so he does. Baynard rejoins Schultz back in the cab as Wells finishes up a conversation with a man he knows. Wells appears through the door and starts walking toward the rig when two women on the porch call out to him and he wheels back to speak with them for a few moments.

"Man, everywhere you go with him, it's like a family reunion," Baynard says of Wells, who does indeed seem to know someone anywhere the crew goes on this side of the city.

Wells finishes with his greetings and returns to the rig, and Schultz steers it to the corner of James and Broadway, where he pulls over to the side of the street so Wells can run into an auto parts store and search for a part they need at the station. As they wait, Baynard spots an automotive repair and body shop on a nearby corner, and the captain takes the opportunity to administer a pop quiz to Schultz.

"Dan," he says, "if there was a fire here, what would you have to worry about?"

Schultz, his arms folded casually over the steering wheel, scans the building for a split-second and spots the large billboard perched atop the shop.

"Heavy load on the roof," he responds matter-of-factly.

"Mm-hm," Baynard nods, "what else?"

Schultz scans the building again.

"No rear exit."

"Mm-hm," Baynard nods again. "Your only way in or out is going to be that front door. I don't know if you can see it, but there are bars on the back window down in the alley, too...What other things would you notice?"Schultz sees that, according to the sign, the business does automotive painting.

"Hazardous materials."

"Right," Baynard agrees. "There's going to be paint in there, and what else goes along with paints? Usually solvents, thinners, lots of hazardous stuff. And because they do auto maintenance, there are going to be oils and other stuff that you've got to worry about. There could be equipment that you'd have to watch for so you wouldn't trip and fall, and there might be a vehicle inside the establishment. So a lot of times when you arrive at a fire, simply by looking at the sign and what kind of establishment it is, you can get all kinds of bells and whistles on what's inside."

It's now Schultz's turn to ask a question, and he asks Baynard how he would have handled being the captain of the second-in engine at the Ascension dorm fire they responded to earlier in the morning. Baynard explains the options he would have considered with regard to the hose sizes and lengths he would have taken into the building in order to have maximum flexibility for finding the fire and attacking it most effectively.

Indeed, whether it's a dormitory with several small rooms and a high occupancy rate, an auto body shop filled with flammable and toxic chemicals, or one of the other thousands of business or residential structures in the city of Minneapolis, firefighters must use their heads before they ever physically go after a fire. It is usually not as simple as, as some firefighters like to put it, putting the wet stuff on the red stuff. Cool-headed thinking and strategizing on a fire scene are required if firefighters are to be able to extinguish a blaze with as little damage to life and property as can be expected.

The engine company is soon back at the station, where the members of the ladder company are watching TV or taking mid-afternoon catnaps. Wells, Baynard, and Schultz eat a late lunch in the dining room, where an old Tony Curtis movie that no one is really watching provides background noise. Once Schultz finishes his meal, he moves to the coop, a small room on the east side of the station that connects the TV room and the apparatus floor. The coop contains the station's computer and an electronic call box that displays emergency calls as they come in. All around the walls, hung in neat rows, are clipboards displaying department communications, policies, and safety instructions, as well as maps of the city's fire wards.

Schultz settles into one of the several office chairs in the room and throws his feet up on a desk and begins reading a fire union newspaper. Above his head hangs a small poster displaying a postage stamp bearing the photo of three New York firefighters raising an American flag at the World Trade Center site. The poster is strapped to the wall with four wide strips of silvery duct tape.

Anderson is in the TV room watching "The Final Conflict," the third installment of an apocalyptic movie trilogy that began with "The Omen." Despite it's chilling storyline on the rise of Satan's son in the world, Anderson is far from spooked. Instead, he laughs loudly and repeatedly at the film's creepiest moments. Schultz, still reading in the coop, chuckles at his colleague's ability to find amusement in what is supposed to be a terrifying story.

But Anderson will not get to see how this one ends, as the fire tones ring out again just after three o'clock, and both Engine 14 and Ladder 10 are soon on the move, racing toward a high-rise apartment building on Lowry Avenue.

This particular apartment high-rise, located at 315 Lowry, is a frequent destination for the companies at Station 14. Located just off the freeway of Interstate 94 and home to a diverse mix of residents, fire alarms at 315 Lowry often turn out, happily, to be false alarms. Anything from a smoke detector being activated to mischievous children pulling fire alarm handles in the hallways to technical malfunctions in the building's alarm system will bring the fire department running. Engine 14 arrives first and pulls through a shallow horseshoe of a driveway in front of the building. There is no sign of smoke or fire, and Baynard radios this information to dispatch.

After Schultz and Baynard jump out and heft hose bundles onto their shoulders, Wells squeezes the engine past a car parked illegally in the fire lane and pulls around to the back side of the building. The car's driver is in the lobby and, once he realizes his vehicle is obstructing the fire lane, comes walking out to move it. He is a young man in his late teens dressed in a bright gold Los Angeles Lakers uniform and has a Lakers hat tilted on his head. But before he can make it all the way down to the sidewalk to his vehicle, Anderson has navigated the massive ladder truck in behind it and, unable to get past, blasts the rig's bellowing air horn as he brings the truck to a stop. The young man slinks the rest of the way to his car and sheepishly climbs in through the front door to get it out of the way. People all over the city routinely park their vehicles in fire lanes, especially when they are only making a quick stop and are certain that the odds a fire engine will actually need the space are slim to none. This driver lost that bet today, and had he not been around to move his vehicle, Ladder 10 would have had to set up further away from the building, costing the firefighters time and energy to get their equipment inside. The extra distance would have made it especially difficult to raise the truck's aerial ladder to upper floors had a ladder rescue been necessary. Lucky for the car's owner, he was near enough to get it out of the way quickly, but not near enough to avoid a deafening admonition from Anderson.

As is usual at this apartment building, the alarm turns out to be a false one set off by a drop in pressure in the pump in the basement that forces water to the building's sprinkler system. Usually a drop in pressure would mean a fire had activated a sprinkler; thus the automatic alert that went out to the fire department. It also set off a cacophony of alarm whistles that is still trilling throughout the building. It turns out the pressure drop was caused by a malfunction of some sort, and Baynard informs dispatch that maintenance is being called in.

In the routine search performed — in full gear, which weighs about 75 pounds — by the firefighters as they arrived, Schultz twisted his right knee slightly while ascending the steps with a bundle of hose draped over his shoulder. As Engine 14 packs up to head for home, Schultz's knee protests, and he winces. It's nothing too major, he thinks, but it feels like one of those tweaks that will nag him for the rest of the shift.

Schultz, Baynard, and Wells return to the station ahead of the ladder company, which has remained on the scene to finish up with routine procedures. But Wells has only just backed the engine into the station when the fire bells ring out again. A call for a burning car has come in from Penn Avenue, and Engine 14 is en route in a matter of seconds. Wells pushes the wailing fire engine south to Lowry and stops momentarily to allow Ladder 10, which is responding east to west from the apartment building, to pass by in front of him before steering on to Lowry himself. Both rigs careen south on Penn while cars scatter to get out of the way.

As the rigs make a right turn on to Broadway, flames and smoke can be seen licking out from a vehicle parked in a small lot behind several houses that are next to a closed and boarded-up Burger King. The ladder truck pulls to a stop on Broadway as the engine pulls into a small stretch of alley that leads closer to the lot where the car is burning. Wells brings the engine to a halt near several discarded window-unit air conditioners that lay in a shattered heap near the old Burger King's drive-thru lane.

The car on fire is a white Chevy sedan, and flames are spouting viciously from underneath the hood. As Schultz begins pulling a line from the engine, Baynard strides confidently toward the madly burning vehicle and disappears into the smoke, appearing on the other side of the vehicle a moment later after ascertaining just how much of car is filled with flame. As he makes his way back toward Schultz and Wells, the latter of whom is now out of the rig and throwing the engine into pump, the car belches a loud puff of steam through its front grill.

A moment later, the right front tire succumbs to the searing heat of the flames and explodes with a deafening boom, and the car sags a bit. The ladder company has made its way across the parking lot to the car, and Caouette begins hammering away at the grill with an axe in an attempt to knock away the latch holding the hood shut. Modahl moves to the rear of the car and goes to work on the trunk with an axe of his own. After a handful of banging swings, the trunk surrenders to Modahl's power and slowly begins to open. He turns and spits. Wells yells out to him from his position at the pump.

"Hey Shawn! What was that, eight swings? That's got to be a new record!"

Modahl juts a gloved fist into the air and turns back to the trunk to see if the flames have reached it and to check for flammable materials or chemicals — a case of engine oil maybe, or a spare gallon or two of gasoline. Anderson and Caouette have now teamed up on the hood, and with one final, powerful slam of Anderson's sledgehammer, the hood lifts up and exposes a crackling mass of flame. Moments later, another deafening boom sounds as the left front tire explodes. A little girl watching from the window of a nearby house screams, but the firefighters, now flanking the car on all sides, don't even seem to notice the noise.

Schultz has pulled his oxygen mask on so that he can delve deeper into the smoke pouring from the car. He moves in close and opens up the inch-and-three-quarter line. The fire gurgles and hisses its irritation at the high-pressure shower, but it quickly banks down as Schultz overwhelms it with the gush of water.

A handful of people have emerged from the house and stand in the dirt yard watching in disbelief at the dramatic scene that has unfolded on their back porch. Wells walks over to the yard to ask the people a few questions. The small girl in the window yells "Hi!" to him, and he waves back.

One of the women tells Wells that she saw a man she estimates to have been in his twenties and wearing a black sweatshirt park the car, get out and walk away, then start running down the alley when flames began poking out from beneath the hood. She doesn't know who the man was or who owns the car. The fire is now on its last leg, and thick smoke banks toward Engine 14, its flashing red lights illuminating the burnt fog. Water pours and drips from underneath the vehicle, its paint and molding on the right side charred black. A gaping black wound in the grill makes the vehicle look like a boxer who has just had his front teeth busted out.

Baynard rips the hood all the way open and flattens it back against the windshield, then orders Schultz to give the motor one final bath of water to make sure any unseen flames are out, as well as to cool the hot metal within, which could otherwise re-ignite any hot gases still swirling inside the vehicle. The arson investigator shows up as the crews are walking back to their rigs. He begins questioning the witnesses as Engine 14 and Ladder 10 take back to the streets.

Both rigs return to the station, then clean and stow the equipment they used at the fire. A short time later, just after five o'clock, Engine 14 is called out to assist someone who is having trouble breathing.

Baynard leads Schultz and Wells into a small house on Queen Avenue, where they find a twenty-four-year-old woman slumped on the floor in front of a couch. Three small girls with braided hair that is filled with multicolored beads are watching stoically near one end of the couch. The woman on the floor tells the firefighters she had her third child five days ago and has been anemic ever since. Her temples are throbbing, she says, and she's short of breath. Schultz provides oxygen for the woman as Baynard gathers as much information from her before the ambulance arrives. The paramedics arrive and take over, and Baynard jokes with the little girls to try and ease their doe-eyed fright.

As the paramedics walk the woman to the ambulance, one of the girls, who looks about three, suddenly transforms into a fount of tears and begins screaming, "Mommy! Mommy!" Another woman in the house tries to calm her down, assuring her that her mommy will be back, but she is still crying as the firefighters leave and close the door.

Back at the station, Baynard meanders into the TV room and finds Anderson watching another of the Omen movies.

"Oooo, Damien," Baynard says with a smile, referring to the movie's main character. "Man, that was the scariest movie I'd ever seen back in the day. I had just read about that mess, and then all of a sudden it was on TV."

Once the movie is over, the viewing becomes much more light-hearted, as Anderson, Caouette, and Schultz settle deeper into their chairs to watch "The Three Stooges." Caouette admits she's never seen an episode before, but is soon doubled over in a fit of hysterical laughter as Larry, Moe, and Curly get on with their slapstick abuse of one another. When Moe falls into a tub of hot rubber, inflates like a balloon, and begins floating away, Anderson and Caouette nearly lose it. Caouette rolls over on her side in the recliner, her face going red with laughter. Anderson's head is thrown back and he gulps great breaths of air while bellowing hysterically. Caouette's glee feeds the hilarity, making Anderson laugh all the more.

"Man, I love it when someone sees the Stooges for the first time!" he booms between gasps of breath.

Shortly before seven, Modahl calls everyone who's in the clutch tonight to the dining room for dinner. "The clutch" is the term for those taking part in the evening's communal supper. One firefighter cooks, and everyone in the clutch pitches in to cover the price of the groceries. Modahl is in charge of cooking today and has whipped up a giant vat of tomato soup filled with tortellini, carrots, and hamburger, served next to a large plate of grilled cheese sandwiches. The firefighters congregate around the two long dinner tables and attack the soup, sandwiches, and large quantities of plain lettuce salad drenched in salad dressing, as well as large cups of water, milk, and soda. Soon the grilled cheese plate is empty, with just a few greasy crumbs left where the mountain of sandwiches so very recently stood. Anderson clanks his spoon into the bottom of his empty bowl — his third helping — and declares it the best soup he's ever had. Modahl quietly absorbs compliments from others, then produces a plate of cinnamon rolls from the kitchen. These, too, are attacked mercilessly by the warm-bellied firefighters. Afterward, everyone pitches in getting the dining room and kitchen cleaned and mopped. Baynard begins wrapping the leftover cinnamon rolls in plastic, and he notices one of them has been partially eaten. He stares at it incredulously for a moment.

"Who did this? Did you do this?" he asks each of the men in the kitchen, his voice raised to compete with the sound of tables and chairs being scooted across tile floor and running water in the kitchen sink. No one claims it, but Rogalski says it looks like Anderson's handiwork.

"Hey, Mark!" Baynard shouts, "Did you do this?"

Anderson turns from rinsing plates in the sink.

"Yep."

Everyone breaks out laughing as Baynard fixes an amused stare on the giant firefighter.

"What! I was saving it for later," Anderson bellows as his station mates continue to razz him. "Who says I have to eat it all at once?" he adds matter-of-factly, then swipes the roll from the plate and takes another bite.

"Plus, I left it on the outside edge so it wasn't touching the others."

He polishes the big roll off with two more bites.

Once the dining room floor dries and the tables and chairs have been put back in place, the firefighters spread out to various corners of the station for the evening. Wells and some of the others are perusing a catalog filled with fire and EMS training manuals when a teenager who lives across the street from the station walks through the door. "T," as he is known around the station, lives with his mother and comes in frequently to chat with Wells, whom he considers something of a father figure. T hopes to be a firefighter one day and, after poring deliberately through the catalog for a minute or two, finds a book that interests him. He says he plans to buy it, but Wells tells him he can get it at the library and should save the money by just checking it out.

"Really? I'm going to go down and get it tomorrow," T says determinedly.

He then asks if anyone has a copy of the firefighting movie "Backdraft" he can borrow to watch. Either VHS or DVD will do. "What do you want to watch those unrealistic fires for?" Wells asks, shaking his head. "There's no smoke, they're not wearing any masks, not even in a haz-mat fire?"

But someone finally says that T can borrow his copy and will bring it in for him next shift. The teen nods with satisfaction and turns his attention back to the catalog.

A few hours deeper into the night, Engine 14 gets a call to a house on Sixth Street. It's for a shooting. Wells, Baynard, and Schultz are soon out the door, and Wells brings the rig to within a block of the incident, where they will stage and wait for police clearance. The cops are descending from all directions. Over the radio, the dispatcher states that three suspects are reported to be driving away toward Lowry, and a squad car peels away from the scene and heads in that direction. The call finally comes in that Engine 14 is cleared to move in. They pull around the corner and up to the front of the house. There does not seem to be much going on, but it soon becomes clear that someone has blasted away with a shotgun inside the front of the house. Witnesses say someone had been hit in the arm, but the wounded person has fled the scene and there is no one for the firefighters to treat.

But they notice there is a heavy odor of natural gas spreading out into the street in front of the house, so Baynard orders Wells to drive down and block off one end of the street and asks the police to seal off the other. Wells radios dispatch for the gas company to send a repair truck to the scene as Schultz and Baynard begin searching around the house for the source of the gas leak.

Wells steers the rig into place to clamp off the flow of traffic about 100 yards away to the south, at the intersection of Sixth and

Lowry. He then walks up and down the street ordering people to get back in their houses. Just after Wells climbs back into his driver's seat, a black and silver sport-utility vehicle pulls out from the curb near the shooting house and begins speeding toward the rig, as if the driver plans to ram his way through.

Just before the vehicle gets to the fire engine, the driver hits the brakes and veers over toward the corner of the intersection and begins yelling out the window for Wells to move the rig and let him through. He is obviously in a big hurry to get out of the area, so rather than wait for Wells to move, he simply plows his way over the curb and accelerates away to the west on Lowry.

A pack of agitated teenagers soon appears from the darkness to the south and begins making its way up the street toward the house where Baynard and Schultz are searching. They are led by one particularly animated youth wearing a skull cap, a shiny blue football jersey and his jeans tugged down to the back of his knees, exposing his boxers. The police turn the teens away from the area, but the kid with the skullcap continues to make unintelligible outbursts to everyone and no one as he leads his cohorts back onto Lowry. His arms flailing as he bobs up and down, the leader walks straight down the middle of the road, forcing startled motorists to take evasive action before the group finally disappears into the night a couple of blocks away.

Baynard and Schultz are walking calmly back toward the rig, the reflective tape on their turnout gear marking their strides on the darkened street. The gas company has arrived, and their maintenance people begin investigating Baynard's assertion that the leak was caused when a fragment from the shooting pierced the gas meter, allowing the firefighters to head for home.

As Wells directs the rig west on Lowry, the firefighters eye the teenagers still milling about in the streets. Here and there a police cruiser is patrolling slowly through the shadows of the side streets.

"We're getting ready to have to come back down here tonight," Wells says.

"Yep, there's some bad blood with someone down here," Baynard replies, then takes another gaze out the window. "Yeah, we may be coming back down here tonight."

ANSWERING THE BELL

It's not long after Engine 14 returns that everyone is in bed. But just after one in the morning, the lights snap on in the upstairs dormitory and the evenhanded tones of a fire alarm jar the drowsing firefighters back to wakefulness. They file out of the bunkroom, which contains twenty-four beds separated by office cubicle partitioning, and slide the pole one at a time.

Engine 14 is out the door first, but as they head west on 33rd, the crew hears a radio transmission from Rogalski that Ladder 10 is out of service and will not be able to make the run. Dispatch announces it's sending Ladder 4 in its place as Wells, Baynard, and Schultz wonder aloud what could have held up their cohorts.

The "fire" turns out to be a tray of smoking cookies, and the responding companies return to their stations. As Wells backs the rig back into the station, Anderson and Modahl can be seen standing near the base of the pole. Caouette sits in a chair next to them, a yellow blanket draped over her shoulders. She did not get a good grip on the pole and free-fell the twenty-six feet from the upstairs floor to the ground below, wrenching her left leg when she hit. Caouette is shaken at how fast the ground rose up to meet her, but feels lucky that she was not more badly injured. A fall of just twelve feet is considered mortally dangerous for a human being, as the impact from a fall from that height can tear the aorta away from the heart.

Her crewmates have wrapped an ice pack around her ankle, and Rogalski is on the red department phone reporting the incident.

Caouette is tough, but she is in lip-biting pain. The muscles in her forehead are tightly drawn, and she is trembling. After saying she thinks she can make it through the night and her crew carries her to bed, the pain becomes too much. Anderson and Modahl suggest she just go to the hospital. Caouette, shaking almost uncontrollably now, agrees. She climbs on to Anderson's broad back and rides piggyback down the steps and into the cab of the truck.

As the rig pulls out into the night with its wounded cargo, Schultz flops down into a chair in the dining room as Wells and Baynard head back upstairs to sleep. Schultz clicks the TV on. His night hasn't been particularly restful to this point anyway, as the knee he twisted earlier in the day aches and made his sleep fitful. He leans back in his seat, contemplating the day gone by. In one shift, his own knee was injured responding to a false alarm, and now Caouette has gotten banged up because someone didn't keep a close enough eye on their midnight snack.

"This job," he states in a thoughtful, measured tone, "can beat you up."

ANSWERING THE BELL

"Look at all these people who needed help."

It's late, almost three in the morning when Elondo Wright utters these words with a quiet reverence, almost an amazement, as he sits in the coop and flips through the pages of the fire department's hand-written logbook.

"*All* these people needed help," Wright repeats. His fingers are turning the pages of the log, one by one. It's in this logbook that the firefighter on house watch records by hand the time each call comes in, the nature of the call, which rigs responded, and so forth. But behind each of these simple entries is someone's personal crisis. Wright briefly and gently smoothes each page with his palm before flipping it over. The pages are curled slightly, bowed by the sheer weight of the ink that covers them, as well as the strength of the hands that have etched the data into place. Fires, breathing problems, drug overdoses, stabbings, strokes, shootings, bone fractures, burns, seizures, abdominal pains; you name it, these, and any other number of ways the human organism can be traumatized, are all recorded on the pages of the logbook.

Wright grew up in a South Side neighborhood plagued by guns and illicit drugs. He was no stranger to death and danger for more of his young life than he would like to remember. But with the stern guidance of his Pentecostal preacher father, Wright eventually found his way out of it all and into a purposeful pursuit in life. Wright has been a member of the fire department for the past four and a half years. He can no longer imagine doing anything else. All he wants to do is help people.

He, like most firefighters, loves his job with a rich intensity. But, oh, there are days — days when the job is neither glamorous nor exciting. Like the time early in his career that he and his engine crew responded to a call and found a small boy whose head had gotten tangled inside his pillowcase while he was sleeping. Wright immediately noticed that the boy's blood had rushed to one half of his body — the half nearest the planet's gravitational pull. That and the bloating told Wright the boy was already dead. Not only did such a young child's death seem maddeningly absurd, but Wright also had to deal with the stoic eyes of the boy's young brothers as they watched from the couch while the firefighters, shoulders slumped a bit, filed heavily out of the room. The snuffing of a young soul was bad enough, but Wright also grieved that the boy's siblings might forever, in the simple and deep-seated way that small minds can, associate the firefighters with their brother's disappearance from their lives.

But Wright and his fellow firefighters, for the most part, find a way to avoid becoming jaded at the sight of death and destruction. Certainly, the number of lives they preserve works as a salve to their big hearts. As long as there are people they can help, they can handle the bad days.

"I think that I've always been a person that takes initiative to help somebody. Even before this job, I always wanted to help somebody, I always wanted to do something," Wright says. "I didn't ever really think about if I wanted to do it at this level, but I know that I've always wanted to be a person that made a difference, even if it's just to put a smile on your face, I've always wanted to do that. But ten years ago, I never thought I'd go into a burning building."

In 1996, Wright was driving buses, pulling down about ten grand a year with three small mouths to feed at home. Things were tough, almost unbearably so, but he realized just how fortunate he was. He could have ended up like Christine, the girl who sat in front of him in class in school. She had gotten involved with the gangs on the South Side and got two bullets in the back of her brain for her trouble. His next-door neighbor was also shot and killed. He knows of at least two other kids from his class who are still around the old neighborhood. One is deeply into drugs, the other in and out of jail. Yes, things could definitely have turned out much worse for a young black man reared on the 4500 block of Portland Avenue South in the late '70s and early '80s.

Things in his old neighborhood are better these days. The gang activity has subsided, and many of the houses there are now filled with hard-working Mexican immigrant families. His father, Author, and mother, Nina, still live in the home where Wright grew up. But as a boy, the house seemed something of a prison to Wright. His father was stern, and as a preacher he insisted his three sons be in by six o'clock every night for prayer time. It was the best way he knew to keep them out of the clutches of thugs that roamed the streets all the more boldly at night. There were no sleepovers at friends' houses, and sports, which so many people — particularly young black men — see as a potential ticket out of the city, were out of the question. His father did not allow Wright to play basketball, even though it was, and remains to this day, one of his passions.

"He said 'If you're good in high school, they'll want you in college,'" Wright recalls with a smile. "'And if you're good in college, they'll want you in the pros. And if you're in the pros, you can't go to church on Sunday.'"

Basketball was just one of the many "worldly things" Author didn't want his sons getting caught up in, but these strictures were not imposed merely for heavenly purposes. The potential to be swept away into the roiling tide of violence that could wash a young black man into the streets was too high, and Author wouldn't allow that to happen. Oh, there were times when Wright and his brothers tried to push it and test their father's limits, but Author would bring his foot down every time, sometimes complete with physical reminders.

"Everywhere it was just gang members, and if it wasn't gang

members it was drug dealers," Wright says. "My dad knew he had three minority kids to raise, so he kept us from doing drugs and he kept us in the church. And he believed in whuppings, so he disciplined us. But all three of my dad's sons are working and we're not in jail. And it's because of our dad. He kept a strong hand and a heavy foot. He said, 'Hey, I don't play that, and that's how it's gonna be.' The writing is on the wall. Everything that he predicted would happen if we followed the straight and narrow came to pass."

There was a firehouse, Station 27, on the way to school, and Wright would walk by it every day and see the big red fire engine and the firemen. They were all fire*men* at the time, and white, at least those that Wright remembers seeing. Wright regarded firefighters with the same simple awe that so many children do, but day after day, year after year, the only firefighters he saw were white. His mind became conditioned to believe he could never join their ranks, simply because of the color of his skin.

"Not even in my wildest dreams, and not even in a little dream, did I think about getting that job, because I thought that's not for me. I mean, I remember thinking that if that job was for me, they'd have people like me on that job."

His words are not bitter, just honest recollections of a young boy on the inside looking for a way out of the urban turmoil around him. In his mind, firefighting was not a potential career for a young black man growing up on the South Side. That's all.

So, after graduating from Washburn High School in 1986, Wright began bouncing from job to job in fast food and retail, wherever he could pick up a paycheck. He was married in 1991, and his first child, Porsha, was born a year later. Two more babies came along in the next four years, and in his first decade after high school, he skipped from menial job to menial job, trying to keep the bills paid and the family off welfare. He was restless in these jobs, and he felt that there was — there had to be — something more for him out there.

Wright spotted a recruitment ad for the Minneapolis Fire Department in *The Spokesman*, a black advocacy newspaper in Minneapolis. The department was in the middle of the process of trying to improve its minority hiring practices. Wright applied, but his imbedded belief that blacks were not allowed to be firefighters warned him off. Something in his own mind simply told him not to expect much. Still, he had seen those firefighters at Station 27 rushing off to help people on his way to school. It was a higher purpose, and he longed to experience it.

"I saw what they were doing," he says, "but I wanted to see how their hearts felt as they were helping someone."

His application was declined.

"But that didn't bother me at all, because nothing's going to hurt if you already expect it."

A short time later he received a letter urging him to apply again, and after a series of interviews and testing, he was accepted to the department on October 21, 1996.

"I used to go to the barbershop and say, 'Man, I'm going to be on the fire department!' and they'd be like, 'They ain't going to let you on there. I don't know why you're wasting your time.' They didn't believe it; they just didn't believe it. But they wish they'd followed me now, because I followed a dream that, really, I shouldn't have followed but I did. To be on the department, it shows a lot of people that if you can really do anything if you put your heart into it."

Wright felt he had finally received his commission in life, and it would be filled with excitement and redeeming value from now on. No more busing tables at restaurants, no more cleaning pubic hairs out of toilets in athletic clubs. He was filled with romantic visions of leaning out of the window of a bright red fire engine as it screamed down the street, and of pulling people from burning buildings. He entered rookie school in 1996 and began his training. Wright's soul was lit up like a four-alarm, high-rise blaze. He felt his life was finally on track after years of flushing the days away at work. He'd finally be able to feel proud of what he did for a living, and he felt his entire family could take pride in him.

Then he was jarred back to a very terrible reality by the very institution that had filled him with so much hope. About halfway through his training, he and a handful of other rookies, all black, were asked to remain in a classroom while the rest of the recruits were ushered away. Wright sensed something was wrong. "I felt like we were pigs waiting to be slaughtered," he recalls.

An officer of the department came in and informed them they were all suspected of being gang members, and were being released from the department. End of story. Wright, who insists he has never been connected with any gang at any time in his life, was devastated.

"At that time, someone felt that gangs were infiltrating the fire department," Wright says. "It bothered me because, even if I was, which I'm not, but if I was a gang member, I'm trying to change my life for the better. And that's what bothered me."

Wright and the others decided to get a lawyer and fight the decision. After a long battle in court, Wright and several of the others were reinstated about two years later. In that time, he had little to hold onto but his faith in God and his deep, deep desire to get this job. Even his father — the preacher man who had instilled in him his faith — advised Wright to cut his losses and let it go. He was further tempted to walk away when the litigants were offered a cash buyout. Two of them took the money and ran, but not Wright. He just felt it in his bones that he had to become a firefighter.

"I wanted to show my kids that a black male could be a respected professional in this society," he said.

Still, Wright was constantly reconsidering his decision to apply at all. Yes, he was able to draw on a deep reservoir of perseverance forged growing up in the heat of a tough neighborhood and unfulfilling jobs that he did not want to go back to. But ultimately his heart sunk at the prospect of being shunned in any way by the firefighters he would be living and working with in the very near future. Deep down, he knew it was unlikely he would run into much discrimination among his front-line comrades, but what if? There could be times when they would be called upon to save each other's lives. It's hard to imagine a more potentially catastrophic time for animosity to bubble up.

Wright also knew he might have to deal with the fact that some of his fellow firefighters might question how he had gotten into the academy in the first place. Was he truly qualified? Was he here just because he was black? Would white firefighting candidates find their road to the department tougher because people of color were receiving preference? Such questions have become needle-sharp points of contention in any discussion regarding affirmative action in any sector of American life, and Wright knew there would be those who would question his very presence.

"In any job they might say, 'You're just in here because of discrimination laws,' or this or that. And when that happens, you really feel like you have to prove yourself more or really get in there, because they don't think you got this job as an equal opportunity, or they think you got this job because you're a person of color. I'm sure some people say it, but they're not blatant about it. But you can tell by some people's actions towards you that they're thinking maybe you took a relative's job. So that's on the department, just like it would be on any other job."

"I did go through it, and I wanted this so bad, but there were times that I was willing to give it up because I thought, you know, if someone doesn't want to work with you or really feel for you like they should, why would you want to work with somebody like that? No amount of money could help you with that."

Things weren't always easy, even after he got into the stations. His wife left him suddenly one day, and she dropped their children off at the station where he was working before driving away. But a short time later he met another woman, Greta, and they would eventually get married and have children together. They are very happily married, he says, adding that she is his biggest supporter and the true love of his life.

Wright is looking only forward now, to a future that holds so much more promise than his past. And yet, one gets the sense that he wouldn't change much, if anything, even if he could. He is like a sword forged in an emotional fire as hot as any he faces on the job. And when a sword emerges from its final firing, any contaminants that sought to invade it and corrupt its core have been seared away, and it is stronger than ever.

"All this stuff happened, and life deals you a hand and you've just got to play your hand the best that you can," he says. "But you know, the department has changed and I love coming to work every day and I love spending time here."

ANSWERING THE BELL

And so Wright comes to work, one of the four firefighters regularly assigned to Engine 14. Some engines in the city run with just three firefighters at a time, but the department tries to keep Engine 14 staffed with four as much as possible. They handle too many stabbing and shooting incidents, at times with multiple victims. An extra pair of helping hands is often necessary on this side of town. A lot of the people look like Wright here, a fact that's not lost on the sturdy firefighter. His own experiences as a kid help him appreciate the service he provides, not only in terms of the duties of his job, but in the way black children perceive firefighters. Or more specifically, their chances of one day becoming one.

"You see black kids that see you and say, 'Hey, someday I can do that job.' Being on that rig, to me, is just like I'm giving hope that I didn't have to someone young."

It's Saturday, and Wright is running a mop across the tile floor in the station's upstairs bathroom on a bright and warm summer morning. Saturday is cleaning day at the fire stations in Minneapolis, and Wright has already bathed the bathroom sinks and toilets in a thick, blue cascade of disinfectant solutions. The air is damp and the fumes from the chemicals cause eyeballs to tighten. Downstairs, the rest of the firefighters are pulling all the equipment off the rigs and scrubbing down the insides of each compartment. Anderson is on the back of the ladder at the base of the aerial mount, his forearms covered to the elbow with a thick, gooey oil as he lubricates the giant ladder. Wright empties out the mop bucket and begins refilling it with fresh water. He can't help but chuckle at everyone who thinks firefighting is always a glamorous job.

"I have *so* many people who say, 'I wish I had your job. I wish I could do what you get to do,'" he says as his mop swishes across the floor.

After about an hour and a half of this, the station is clean and the rigs have been freshly scrubbed and are drying in the sun on the front driveway. The dull film of dust has been washed away and their red shells gleam. The rest of the morning is quiet. After noon, messy gray clouds move in and begin blotting out the blue sky.

The neighborhoods on the North Side are dotted with abandoned houses. Every few blocks in many of the neighborhoods, there is at least one house with boarded up doors and windows. Many have abandonment papers stuck to them with duct tape, while others bear bright orange notices that payments for the waste and water services are delinquent, and the services will soon be shut off. It's the fire department's job to make a sweep through the area every week to make sure none of these houses have been broken into and occupied illegally or, worse, turned into fire hazards. So a little after noon, Wright, Jay Wells, and Captain Tim Baynard are getting ready to set out and do the inspections.

Baynard is tall with long, powerful arms and a smart mustache. A frost of white across his hairline lends a professorial air to his otherwise youthful appearance. He and Wright will jump off the rig at most of the houses to take a quick walk around, but the service they provide to the community while making their rounds today will be of a far more dynamic nature than simply making sure plywood barriers haven't been pried away. All of the firefighters on the rig are black, and their interaction with the residents in the area will further strengthen the bonds between the firehouse and the locals.

Wells rolls Engine 14 a few feet out of the station and stops for a moment while Wright finishes with some last-minute duties. A woman with a pitted face and long, straight, black hair saunters past the firehouse. She is wearing an ill-fitting little black number. Her eyes are set straight ahead, but it seems clear she knows the firefighters are there and wishes to catch their eye. They see her but pay little attention. She disappears up the street, but just fifteen seconds later she comes walking back down in the other direction, just as casually as before. Wells and Baynard do their best to ignore the woman, who is so obviously strutting for them. Soon she has passed, however, and with Wright now on board, Wells steers the fire engine south onto James.

The rig has not rolled half a block when a man in his front yard swiftly scoops up his small daughter and points to the big red fire engine rumbling docilely towards them. The little girl freezes in her daddy's arms and appears awed, so Captain Baynard flashes a warm smile and gives her a quick wave.

They make their way south of Lowry, where the houses are older and appear to sag under the humid air and the weight of their own roofs. Few of these homes have much, or any, air conditioning, so their residents have started spilling out onto the front stoops to wile away some time in the fresh, albeit sticky, air. Many of them wave or shout to the firefighters, who return the salutes with nods and smiles of their own. Here, on some of the poorest streets in the city, the mere presence of black firefighters seems to buoy people's spirits. Blank faces that have been staring out into the street for hours suddenly flicker when they see the firefighters with skin as darkly hued as their own. Children jump and dance on hardscrabble front lawns when the engine approaches. All wave, and others pump their fists in the air, signaling frantically for Wells to honk the engine's air horn. The firefighters in their trim, navy blue dress uniforms and massive red fire engine offer hope to folks from this part of the city that they too can be productive, accepted, trusted with great civic responsibility in their own communities.

Here and there, the rig rolls past one or two young black male teenagers dressed in baggy shorts and T-shirts that hang off their lanky shoulders. It is early afternoon, but the youths drag themselves sleepily down the street, looking as if they have just emerged from a long night of hard revelry. They are boys becoming men, but they have a hard and uncertain road ahead of them. Thin strips of muscle are forming on their lean limbs, but even as their bodies are burgeoning, a lot of them see their prospects in life atrophying. They are about to enter their last few years of school, knowing that a steep precipice awaits them once they graduate, if they graduate. A lucky few will head off to college, but many others will find themselves fighting against the current of drugs and petty crime that swirls around their feet, threatening to pull them down into a morass from which they might never escape. It is through bleary eyes that these youths watch vacantly as Engine 14 rolls by.

The firefighters are glad to see that some of the abandoned

houses are receiving new coats of paint and might soon be occupied again. But many need a lot of work. A fat, blue pigeon eyes the rig from a broken second-story window as it rolls by. A small Asian boy who looks no older than five sits motionless, chin resting on his hand, on the ground next to his scooter under a sign that reads "Dead End Alley." Some yards and alleys are littered with old boxes, outdated stereo equipment, and other trash, but many others are green and lush. Several old tires lie in one yard, while in another, three tires have been painted white and turned into flowerboxes with cheery red flowers poking out of the middle.

Wells abruptly stops the rig in front of one house and yells out the window to a heavyset woman sitting alone on her porch. He asks how she is feeling. At first she seems confused that someone is shouting in her direction, but her face lights in recognition, and she says she's feeling better. Across the street, while Wells continues his conversation in the other direction, three children that appear to be between the ages of four and six wave through a smudged glass door, while a girl in the adjoining window shouts, "Hi firemen!" over and over. Another wave from the firefighters as they drive away stokes their glee.

As they make their way back toward Lowry, a small boy squirts pink cleaning fluid at the fire engine, aiming for the rolled-down windows. A few seconds later, Wright points out a house where a child hurled a rock at them several days ago. The big red truck is, it seems, an irresistible moving target for some of the children confined to these small yards in cramped neighborhoods. But for the most part, these children are overjoyed to see these big men with black faces riding high in the big rig as it squeezes its way down the streets.

Two Asian women are selling produce on a street corner, right next to a tent where a vendor is selling Christian-themed T-shirts. The engine company from Station 16, located along the southern edge of the North Side, is sitting in the adjacent parking lot. Wells pulls Engine 14 to the curb, and he, Wright, and Baynard hop out and begin chatting and joking on the street corner with the trio of firefighters from their fellow North Side station.

Keith "Big Hungry" Blasingame is the captain on Engine 16

today. Big Hungry is a shorter man with a thick torso and a pleasant face, and he is clutching a pair of candy bars that he just bought from a young girl who's raising money for charity. He has been on the department for five years. He likes the work on this side of town, even though it's not as busy since the city tore down the projects that provided Engine 16 with plenty of work. With sons at both Patrick Henry and North high schools in Minneapolis, he is hoping to set an example, providing a beacon that his boys can follow as they prepare to step into a real world of harsh realities.

"I just want them to be productive," Big Hungry says.

Big Hungry plunges in with the other firefighters, who are razzing each other over a recent bowling outing together. He reminds the men of Engine 14 that if they get called to help on a fire in Engine 16's territory today, they won't see much action, as they will have it put out before they get there. In mock retaliation, Baynard confiscates one of Big Hungry's two candy bars and begins eating it. Big Hungry just smiles as he revels in the wash of laughter from his comrades. This camaraderie is what makes the department so attractive to many firefighters, but Big Hungry also knows that the levity can turn to dead seriousness in an instant if the call box on either rig goes off.

"It can all change, like this," he says, running his hand quickly past his face, like a mime switching from happy to serious.

A few minutes later, Engine 14 is rolling again. It's midafternoon and the gray clouds are starting to spit. The rig pulls into a local church where a small parking lot carnival is being held. The department has agreed to send the fire engine over for the kids to see. A bespectacled man in a bad tuxedo is doing magic tricks under an open, wind-blown tent, and one by one heads turn away from his magic top-hat as they see that the fire engine has parked nearby. Half of the magician's audience disappears in a flash as the children realize the big red truck is here for them, and they climb over each other in glee to get their chance to touch it, sit in it, just be near it. Wright tries to shape the bubbling mob of kids into some semblance of a line, then climbs onto one of the chrome steps and begins helping the kids into the fire engine's cab, one at a time.

The children are overjoyed as they sit in the oversized seat, but they grow even more excited when an alarm comes in over the call box. They suddenly have a front-row view of the action, and they watch in awe as their heroes spring into action, pulling on boots and slamming big metal doors behind them as they climb into the cab. Two cars have crashed into each other at a nearby intersection, and the sirens wail as Engine 14 pulls out of the church parking lot and zooms north. An ambulance from North Memorial falls in behind them, and they scream up the street together for the last few blocks.

Wells brings the engine to a halt at an angle in the street, shielding an old, faded, blue sedan that sits in the intersection, its front end smashed. Parked near the curb is a brightly-painted sports coupe with a large gash in the passenger door. Thick strips of white, cottony insulation and thin wisps of black plastic that look like shreds of a garbage bag are hanging out of the coupe's door where a chunk of panel is missing. That hunk of panel is now hooked to the blue sedan's front bumper.

Wright and Baynard hop from the rig and quickly check with each car to see if anyone is injured, while Wells retrieves first-aid equipment from the rig. It is still raining, and the fire engine's warning lights blink off the wet pavement like tiny lightning flashes. Sitting in the old sedan are two elderly women who appear unharmed and entirely calm. Baynard asks if they are hurt at all, and the woman in the passenger's seat replies that they are both fine. She explains that she didn't have her seatbelt on, but was able to brace herself with her hands on the car's dash. She goes on to explain that she even had time to turn around and catch her freshly prepared fruit salad, which was sitting in the backseat. Baynard can't help but chuckle at the old lady's pluck. Despite the fact that the vehicle in which she was riding had just broadsided another car, she had the presence of mind to keep her fruit salad from spilling onto the floor.

The driver of the coupe is a Hispanic girl who appears to be in her late teens. She is out of the car and walking around, talking on a cell phone. She doesn't have any injuries. She comes over to speak with the firefighters and says she doesn't want to get the old ladies in trouble, but that it was the sedan that caused the wreck. An eyewitness agrees, but Wright tells them the police will have to handle that information when they arrive. A squad car eventually shows up, and a balding, gray-haired police officer emerges and walks to the intersection. He immediately recognizes Wright and the two strike up a conversation. The cop had been to Wright's North Minneapolis home the previous day — by mistake. Someone had phoned in a call to 911 that a man in Wright's neighborhood was trying to kill his ex-wife, but it was at a house on the other side of the street. The officer throws his arm around Wright's shoulder, and they laugh about the mixup.

The police begin gathering information on the accident, and the firefighters climb back onto the engine and loop around the block to head back to the church where the carnival is being held. A black sport-utility vehicle zooms up on one side and squirts between the moving rig and a parked car. Baynard hits the driver with a blast from the air horn. It doesn't seem to faze the driver in the least, and the firefighters shake their heads as the SUV runs a red light at the next intersection. The accident scene they just left was apparently caused by a mental lapse on the part of one of the drivers, and it's reckless people like the man driving the SUV that are the cause of so many other potentially deadly collisions.

Only about a half-hour has elapsed from the time Engine 14 tore out of the church parking lot to the time it returns. The rain has tapered off now and the sun is peeking through the clouds. The kids also brighten and come running back toward the fire engine — their earlier enthusiasm easily rekindled. They begin lining up — and cutting in line — to get their turn on the rig. One little boy is crying, startled at being jostled around by the other children, so Baynard kneels to comfort him. The boy calms immediately.

There are a lot of children crowding around the rig, and Wright is realizing it will take more time than they have to get through all of them if he doesn't speed things up. So he climbs onto a step and announces loudly that each child will get to sit in the seat for five seconds, and then they may enjoy the rest of their day. The children giggle, and Wright begins helping them into the seat one at a time.

"Wait, wait, wait, little man," Wright says to one little boy who is having a hard time waiting his turn. "Come on, little mama, time's up," to a girl who doesn't want to leave just yet.

Baynard draws some of the heat off of Wright by inviting a few of the boys in line to come to the rear of the rig. He pulls out one of the hoses and shows off the big gray nozzle with its pistol-grip handle. The boys take turns hefting it, impressed with its weight. One little girl has snuck around to the other side of the rig, and she's rewarded for her resourcefulness by Wells, who lifts her into his driver's seat and snaps a picture for her.

Some twenty minutes later, with the sky clouding over rapidly and winds picking up, the carnival organizers begin tearing down the tents and people scatter for home to seek shelter from the impending rains. The crew says its good-byes to the children, and Engine 14 rolls back into the street to head for home. None of the children were left unsatisfied, and the department's bond with one small corner of the community has been further strengthened. Climbing onto the fire engine was obviously a rare treat for many of the thirty or so kids on hand, and you can bet you won't see any of them hurling a rock when a fire engine zooms by their house in the future.

By four-thirty it is raining again, and now the hail joins in, a barrage of ice pellets bouncing off the engine as it rolls through the streets north of the station. The alarm box sounds — a fire alarm at 315 Lowry, the high-rise apartment building notorious for false alarms. Wells switches on the sirens and spurs the rig on while Wright and Baynard begin pulling on their boots, turnout coats, air tanks, and helmets. Over the radio they hear that Ladder 10 is also en route. As Engine 14 screams south towards Lowry, its big wheels send plumes of rainwater that has collected on the street spraying in both directions. Wells turns the rig onto Lowry and heads east. He pulls into the apartment building parking lot in time to see the crew from Ladder 10 disappear through the front doors. No smoke or flame is showing from any of the tall building's windows.

Wells drops Wright and Baynard in front of the building, and they grab bundles of folded hose and head in. Just inside the door, a security guard and several teenagers are milling about while the building's fire alarms scream. Caouette and Anderson are already on the scene with Ladder 10 and appear from around a corner. It turns out to be another rather harmless scenario. A resident on the sixteenth floor burned a chicken she was cooking for dinner and opened her apartment door to let the smoke out. It either set off a sensor or someone saw the smoke and pulled an alarm.

Eight firefighters in full gear, toting axes, hoses, and other tools suddenly seem like overkill. But they know it is part of the routine. Oftentimes when they are called, the fire department finds someone crying wolf, even if it is inadvertent. But no matter how many false alarms they receive, the firefighters will never stop coming when the bell rings, because they know that many times they will indeed find a wolf waiting for them, a big, blazing red wolf with long flickering tongues trying to devour everything, and everyone, around it. But not this time; just some scalded poultry and one embarrassed amateur chef.

The rain has stopped and the clouds have beaten a hasty retreat, pulling back to reveal a shimmering early-evening sky. Wells steers Engine 14 back toward the north and soon pulls the rig to the curb and parks. The firefighters slide out of their seats and onto the glistening wet grass and begin walking toward one of the small neat houses on the block — the one with several clusters of red and blue balloons tied to the chainlink fence.

This is the home of Terry Pettis and his family. Pettis will soon be leaving for college at Fresno State University. He was perhaps the best senior basketball player in the state of Minnesota this past winter as he led Patrick Henry High School to its third consecutive state title on the hardcourt. Today's festivities are a celebration for one of the neighborhood's shining sons, and the local firefighters have been invited.

They make their way past the side of the house into the backyard where many people are sitting and eating. The firefighters are quickly ushered into the kitchen, and empty plates are placed in their hands. The adjoining room is filled with people, their tone merry and full of laughter. The firefighters heap their plates with barbecued ribs, chicken, red beans and rice, and a variety of salads. Back outside, they make their way through the backyard, where about a dozen women are holding court under a large tent that still drips from the rains that have blown off to the east. They wave and smile their hellos to the firefighters as they march toward the back-alley garage where most of the men have gathered.

In the garage, several men sit at fold-up card tables eating from paper plates and smoking cigarettes. Hip-hop and R&B tunes spill from an old portable stereo that sits on the trunk of an old white Buick that is missing its rear window. Several other men, including Terry's father, are standing and eating, and they heartily welcome the firefighters into their circle. Wells, a huge local hoops fan and North High devotee, and some of the others are soon verbally jostling over which city team will be more dominant next year, which summer leagues are most powerful, and all manner of other topics relating to city basketball. Some of the other men also chime in from time to time, but mostly they just laugh and smoke their cigarettes while Wells and Pettis' father go at it.

"Look at all the players Henry is losing." "North's only got one player coming back." "Maybe two." "Henry's got no big guys." "What? They got Walls. They got Steven." "But they ain't gonna have Terry, and Terry is the reason they did what they did this year." "All right." "Know what I'm saying?" "All right." "Now, North, this year is the year." "Aw, come on." "Just watch." "They've got Kammron. Who else?" "And they ain't got the size." "We're going to sweep this year." "What?" "Hey, y'all lost to South last year." "That was a night after a big game. Just a letdown." "Well, we're gonna sweep this year." "Aw no. Henry will sweep. They got that deep, deep will to win."

Terry arrives in the garage wearing well-pressed denim shorts that cover most of his legs and a Dallas Mavericks jersey over a white T-shirt, Air Jordan shoes and a white headband. He is young, wiry and vigorous, and with his active facial expressions and sprawling grin, he is clearly his father's son. He enters the debate, but for only a short time, then retires back to the house.

Shortly, the firefighters decide to return to the station. They thank their hosts, and as they file back through the yard, the women clap and cheer. The firefighters smile and wave back.

Back to the station at just before six o'clock, and several of the firefighters sit down at the table for dinner. Rogalski, Caouette, Anderson, and Baynard chat and joke while wolfing down bowlfuls of salad and great slithering mounds of spaghetti covered with marinara sauce and Italian sausage. They are about halfway through dinner when a call comes in for Engine 14.

Baynard hops from his chair and bursts through the door to the apparatus floor while the truckies continue with their supper and conversation. Wells emerges from the coop, and Wright slides down the pole to join them on the rig. Wells hits the lights and sirens and the rig tears through the open doors and into the streets. Heading east, they quickly reach a house on Lyndale, where someone has reported that a woman is having trouble breathing. A stocky black man wearing a white undershirt and shorts is waiting on the sidewalk, and he calmly waves the firefighters in.

The house is small but nicely furnished, and a half-dozen small children sit on a couch watching TV, seemingly unaffected by either the sirens or the appearance of the three large firefighters who parade straight through their viewing area. The man directs the trio upstairs and, halfway up, they meet a heavyset young black woman with the tips of her hair frosted blonde. She is in a state of near hysteria and panting with fear as she directs the calm firefighters to the room at the top of the steps, first door on the right.

They enter a small room that apparently belongs to one of the children downstairs. There is a small bed and couch, and the floor is covered with toys. A team photo of the Minnesota Vikings hangs at an angle on the wall, just above the couch where another young woman has collapsed. She is half-kneeling, half-sitting on the floor. Doubled over in pain, her tightly drawn face is pressed into the cushions. Lying near her bare feet on the hardwood floor is an asthma inhaler and a small toy fire engine.

The panicky woman explains that the ailing woman, Annie, recently had a cyst removed from her lower back. She had been complaining that she wasn't feeling quite right, that something was "backing up" into her body. Then they noticed that her stomach had begun to bloat. Annie asked to be taken to the hospital when she lost control of her breathing. After taking a puff of the medicine in her inhaler, she collapsed.

Wells works to calm the hysterical woman, as she is becoming increasingly unnerved. He sternly but calmly informs her that she's not helping the situation, and she finally heads downstairs — her body still trembling — to let the firefighters do what they're here to do.

Baynard is kneeling near Annie, talking loudly but politely to her, trying to assess her awareness of her surroundings while Wright prepares the oxygen and fits the breathing mask over her nose and mouth. Two paramedics arrive, and Annie nods when asked if she can make it downstairs to the ambulance. Wright and Baynard slowly pull her to her feet and help her gingerly down the first few steps. Her strength begins to give out and she begins to tense up and thrash in a state of mild panic. Wright, who is backing down the narrow staircase in front of Annie, peers directly into her eyes.

"If anything happens, we've got you," he says, his gaze locked into hers. "We've got you, okay?"

Annie relaxes, but her strength is gone, and the firefighters lift her completely off the floor and carry her down the steps and into the living room. The children on the couch are still blithely watching television as the firefighters carry the woman through the living room and outside. Annie is soon in the ambulance and headed toward the hospital, and Engine 14 heads for home.

The only other call this day, aside from a false alarm later in the night, came when Engine 14 was at the grocery store. Wright was eyeing fried chicken at the deli in the rear of the store when Wells called out his name from near the front door. Wright sprinted up an aisle and through the door to the waiting rig. Several bystanders, including four teenage boys on their bicycles, watched with curiosity as the fire engine zoomed away. After tending to a year-old baby who was having trouble breathing — and its frightened mother — the firefighters returned to the store. The four boys on their bikes were still there, and they pedaled over to the firefighters, who were walking back in to complete their shopping.

"You guys back from the fire already?" asked one of the thin black youths.

"Nah. No fire," Wells replied.

"No fire?"

"No. Just a medical run."

"You guys do medical runs? Was someone hurt?"

"Nah. It was all right."

A pause. One of the boys, his head tilted and eyes narrowed thoughtfully, jutted his chin into the air.

"You guys are life-savers, huh?" he declared.

Wells laughed. "Is that what we are?"

"Yeah, you guys are life-savers."

Wells turned and walked into the store.

"Nah," he said, not looking back. "I'm just a black man living in Minneapolis."

"One of things I love about this job is you put on your gear, you put on your helmet and mask, and you don't know if it's a woman or a guy. It just doesn't matter."

So says Julie Caouette, one of two women on the regular eight-person A crew at Station 14. These days, when you see a Minneapolis fire engine rolling through the streets, chances are good that you can spot at least one woman somewhere on board. While many cities have only a token woman or two, or no women at all, on their fire departments, nearly a fifth of the firefighters in Minneapolis are female. There are some stations that have reputations for being male-oriented, but women have taken on a much-expanded role in the department in the past few years.

Still, few vocations have the stamp of maleness imprinted on them as thoroughly and profoundly as firefighting. For starters, most people still call them fire*men*. But more to the point, firefighting is a rugged job that often requires long, sustained applications of brute physical strength that, generally, men are better able to exert than women. While it is true that some eighty percent of the fire department's calls annually are of a medical nature that firefighters of either gender can suitably handle, and while it is also true that firefighters do not find themselves hefting two-hundred pounds of unconscious human dead weight over their shoulders as often as Hollywood would have us believe, there do come times when firefighters have to be able to do some extremely heavy lifting, oftentimes with someone's life or death in the balance. Male and female firefighters are held to the same physical standards in training and periodic tests known among firefighters as "Ironmans," but even Caouette and many of her fellow female firefighters acknowledge that most members of the general public probably believe, deep down, that men are at least slightly better equipped to deal with the rigors of firefighting. If a person's property is burning before his or her eyes, or worse, if a loved one is trapped within a flaming building, that person will likely desire that the strongest and swiftest human beings available be sent in to do the rescuing. And the strongest and swiftest human beings, in most people's perceptions of reality anyway, are usually men. Therefore, a fire engine filled with women might be seen as cause for extra concern for anyone whose blood is already charged with the anxiety that comes with seeing your personal belongings being devoured by angry and fast-moving flames.

But firefighting is not quite as simple as charging into a burning building with axes swinging and hoses gushing. At most working fires, not only do firefighters perform search and rescue, they also run and monitor the diesel-powered pumps on the engines, unfurl and position hoses, ventilate burning floors and rooftops, seek out a fire's origin, and develop strategies for attacking the fire with water power. All are tasks that women can often perform as satisfactorily as their male counterparts.

In the eyes of her own crew, whose corporate effectiveness depends on the capabilities of its individual parts, Caouette is more than able to perform the tasks required to effectively fight fire. Ask the male colleagues that share Ladder 10 with her, and they will tell you. Caouette is a good firefighter.

Now in her fourth year on the department, Caouette feels at home at Station 14. She grew up the youngest of four children in a middle-class household over on Vincent Avenue, not far from the station. Just down the street from Station 14 is the store where she had her graduation pictures taken. She frequented the library on

Lowry as a child. Down on Broadway is the store where she bought her school shoes each year. Life in North Minneapolis rolled along relatively pleasantly for much of the early part of Caouette's life, but her parents' divorce during her senior year at Totino-Grace, a Catholic high school in nearby Fridley, shook her sense of stability in the world. Directionless after graduating, Caouette followed the advice of her brothers and enrolled at the University of Minnesota-Duluth. Over the next seven years she worked, took classes, and got married at the age of twenty-two.

Never having achieved a college degree, Caouette moved with her husband to Grinnell, Iowa when he inherited a company whose main factory was in the small college town that sits just off Interstate 80 between Des Moines and Iowa City. For the five months before she settled into Grinnell, Caouette moved to Alaska to work in the fisheries, where she gutted and processed catches of black cod, herring, salmon, halibut, and red snapper. It was hard, smelly, labor-intensive work, and Caouette roughed it in a tent for the entire six months she was there.

After moving back to Grinnell, where her husband joined the town's volunteer fire department, Caouette taught preschool for a time and tested her entrepreneurial skills by running a yarn store for four years. Then it was back to Alaska and the fisheries for a short while before her husband's company was bought out and he landed a job in Atlanta. The couple moved to Georgia and built a house, but the marriage was on its last leg, and they divorced after eight years together.

Caouette was on her own, and she started picking up carpentry skills to support herself. She thoroughly enjoyed the two years she spent using her hands as building tools, and was finding she had a taste for physical labor. Her limbs and back grew strong in the process of throwing up structures, and the raw wood floors she built under her own feet instilled in her an emotional sturdiness, a sense that she was contributing something to the world.

But she soon found herself drawn back to the Midwest. She couldn't afford to live in Minneapolis with its higher cost of living, so she returned to the small-town life in Grinnell. But uprooting herself again further tore at Caouette's confidence. She sensed her life was wandering away on her, that she might never put down roots. In Grinnell, she lived with friends who took her in, and she spent a year doing some carpentry, doing odd jobs at the local private college, and working as a butcher. But a less transient future finally began to crystallize for Caouette when she joined up with her ex-husband's old mates and became the first female on the Grinnell Volunteer Fire Department.

All of the male firefighters with whom she worked had at least five years of experience on the job, which gave them a deep vein of experience for their newest member to tap, and tap it Caouette did. New firefighters are typically more gung-ho than their older counterparts and revel in carrying out even the most routine tasks. And because she was the lone neophyte on the department, she had little competition when it came to throwing herself completely into the various aspects of the job. The veteran firefighters allowed her to jump in with both feet and were there to guide her through each step, and misstep. The town's proximity to I-80 meant lots of automobile and semi wrecks, which provided Caouette with plenty of experience with the Jaws of Life, a cutting tool that looks like a giant set of paring scissors with a thick cylindrical motor attached at the handle. And fires in rural areas were often spotted only after they had gotten out of hand. This gave the firefighters plenty to do once they arrived. And as Caouette soaked in the finer points of attacking fire, her fellow firefighters encouraged her at every turn.

"They said I had more enthusiasm for the job than my ex-husband," she recalled. "They were great. They just gave me a lot of confidence."

After two years of proving herself and fine-tuning her skills on the job, her mentors encouraged her to apply for openings on the small unit of full-timers that manned the station professionally. But she also got word from her mother, still living in Minneapolis, that her home city was hiring for its own fire department. Her mother and boyfriend at the time urged her to apply. Caouette realized it was going to be hard for her to make a life for herself in Grinnell, so, with the additional allure of working for a big-city fire department tingling in her mind, she packed up, returned to her hometown, and applied to become a Minneapolis firefighter. But it can take years before an applicant is ultimately hired by the department, and she needed something to do in the meantime. So she kept herself in shape prior to and during the application process by doing trench work. Putting in water lines and storm sewers, while hardly a glamorous prelude to taking on one of the world's most romanticized jobs, fed her enthusiasm for manual labor and infused her muscles with an extra measure of vigor that would be required in her rookie school training. Caouette eventually got the call she had been waiting for, and she was tapped to enter the department's next rookie academy. Five months later, she realized her goal and was assigned to Station 14 for her first stint as a rookie. She reported for her first day on the job just after the first of the year in 1999.

After a dozen years of floating through life, Caouette's future lay in front of her, as bright, well-grounded, and upward-reaching as the fire pole she would soon be sliding at the old firehouse. But, just as she was set to step heartily into her new profession, her past reared up and refused to let her move on without a fight. She still owed thousands in legal fees from her divorce, and her creditors wanted their money. Determined to get them paid off, and too independent now to move back in with family, she saved money by renting out a small office space for four-hundred dollars a month and making that her home. She put her carpentry skills to work and dressed up the office with a desk she'd built out of an old solid oak door. Her computer doubled as her TV, and a couch and a handful of other hand-made accoutrements rounded out her short list of luxuries. She slept on the floor on a sleeping bag, which she rolled up and stored under a coffee table each morning. There was a bathroom in the hall with only a toilet and a sink, so she had to wait until the beginning and end of each shift at the firehouse to shower. After her first half-year at Station 14 and an equivalent stint on a swing crew — one that splits time between two stations — at Stations 1 and 16, she had enough money to move into an apartment in Hopkins. And just in time, as the owners of the office space had caught on to her living arrangements and informed her that they were not acceptable.

ANSWERING THE BELL

Once her bills were paid off, Caouette was free to focus on growing as a firefighter. Like most new firefighters, Caouette felt she was always being forced to prove herself throughout her first couple years on the department. She began to wonder if she was being put to the test so often by her colleagues because she was a woman, but it didn't take her long to realize that all the other firefighters around here — male and female — were being held to the same high standards.

"The first year, I was kind of thinking that all this stuff is happening to you because you're a female firefighter, like people aren't talking to you or giving you a fair shake. It's something that I think all the women think they have to go through," Caouette says. "But then someone pointed out to me that everyone goes through these things, and they go through them in their own way. If you step back from thinking it's because you're a girl and being defensive, it's a lot easier. In this department now, I think for most people it's not a shocker anymore to have women on with them. Some people still want to hold on to that guys-only mentality, but you just kind of stay away from them a little bit. It'd really be easy for me as a woman to say my troubles in life and on this job are because I'm a woman. It's harder to step back and say it has nothing to do with me being a woman, and this is just how the job is. It's easier to play the victim."

One station in town is known for being a men's only station, and some of the firefighters there carry themselves with an attitude that they're the city's best and baddest. But in most cases, it's not until individual firefighters go to work with their crews at the scene of a fire that it can be determined who passes muster. And, like in any other profession, each person is found to have strengths and weaknesses, and in many cases gender has nothing to do with it. If firefighters, male or female, prove they have what it takes, others around them will take notice. Caouette recalls one moment early in her career that gave her crew the confidence that she could do the job.

She was driving Engine 1 in the heart of downtown Minneapolis for the first time. The rest of her crew was experienced and she admired them as good workers. They kidded her — as most young firefighters are kidded — about her ability to hack it on the job. It was two-thirty in the morning and they were on their way home from a medical run when a fire call came in. A set of apartments above a mountaineering shop in the Cedar-Riverside area near the University of Minnesota was ablaze. Had Engine 1 been back at quarters, it would likely have been the second engine company in, behind Engine 7. But because it was already out on the streets, Engine 1 ended up first on the scene.

A driver's job does not end after he or she successfully navigates the rig to the fireground. It is vital that the driver position the apparatus in a spot that allows its crew to most effectively battle the fire, as well as give arriving engine and ladder companies space to connect and coordinate with the first-in crews. For example, if the first-in engine sets up directly in front of a house that's burning, the ladder will not have a good place from which to base its aerial operations. Or if the first-in engine has its nose facing in the wrong direction, the second-in company may have trouble getting itself in position to relay water to the first engine from a hydrant down the block. A poor decision on the part of first-in drivers can have a domino effect that screws up an entire scene.

When Engine 1 arrived that night, smoke was billowing so heavily into the street that they couldn't even determine for sure where the fire was raging. They thought it might be coming from a nearby bank, but a police officer directing traffic pointed them in the right direction. Caouette swiftly steered the fire engine down an alley to a parking lot behind the store. The captain and another firefighter jumped from the rig and went into the burning building with a line to find the fire. As the driver, it was Caouette's job to get the water pumping. She charged the line when she got the word from the captain over her radio, and her crew went to work attacking the blaze inside. The second-in engine had arrived by this point and was running a supply line to Engine 1 from the hydrant. Caouette continued to tend to her pump and switched over from her own water tank to begin sending water into the building from the hydrant. She also had to keep the engine cooled with circulating water, and make sure the massive pump was drawing and supplying water through the hose at all times.

ANSWERING THE BELL

After the flames had been brought under control and the mopping up operations were beginning, some of the second-in companies began to pack up to head for home. The second-in engine disconnected the hydrant out on the front street, but no one informed Caouette that Engine 1 would soon be losing its water source. Over his radio, her captain informed Caouette that their water pressure was flagging, and she quickly discerned that her supply had been cut. And a pump that's not getting enough water begins pulling in air. Too much air can create a vacuum that causes an entire fire engine to collapse in on itself. So Caouette nimbly switched the water feed back over to Engine 1's own internal water tank, allowing her crew to continue with its washdown and averting potentially disastrous, and expensive, damage to the fire engine. On her first job as the driver of a first-in engine company, Caouette had shown poise, awareness, and a well-developed knowledge of the procedures for setting up to attack a fire that had gone all the way to two alarms. And her crew noticed.

"It was really awesome," she recalls. "While I'm not always the best at explaining academic things when they'd asked me about it, I'm good at physical work and I just know how to do it. So my captain was suddenly a little different towards me. Next time I was driving, there were fewer casual jokes about being unsure about me. Now it was more us joking about another crew or something."

Caouette has also proven herself to the members of her current crew at Station 14, and they have proven themselves to her. But these things aren't just decided at fire scenes. Most firefighters who want their colleagues to know they'll work hard at crunch time display a strong work ethic around the station, doing their share to keep the living quarters and apparatus floor clean and in good repair. There are few places to hide when it comes time to pitch in and help out around a fire station, and if you take it easy when the other men and women are expending their own elbow grease, they'll notice. And they'll remember when you're at a fire. Mark Anderson has been doing this job at the city's busiest stations for more than a decade, and his instincts for how hard someone works are well honed. He can be hard on people who don't give it their all on the job. Conversely, if you do your fair share, it is easy to earn his loyalty. So it is with most firefighters.

"If the person's working and getting along with others in the house, Mark's going to help that person win at fires, even if they're not able to do as much as some of the bigger guys," Caouette says.

With so many relatively new firefighters on the department and the vibrant attitudes they bring with them, there are not a lot of problems with people not pulling their weight. If anything, there sometimes seems to not be enough work to go around, as crews arrive on the scene eager to go straight to work. It is a taboo in the fire service to be caught standing around and allow another crew to step in and perform your task, or worse, commandeer your tools or hose. Most firefighters rue being labeled as part of a slacker crew. And at bigger fires where incoming and fresher crews might be overly eager to elbow their way in and spell the crews that have been working, competition can be fierce when it comes to who gets to do the work.

On occasion, male firefighters have been known to be more likely to try and snatch work away from female firefighters than from other men, but that is something that Caouette rarely has to experience if Anderson is around. There have, in fact, been occasions when he has swept others out of the way to let Caouette get in on the action.

"Mark is usually right there to push me in," she says. "He definitely, definitely looks out for me. And I don't mind. I'm flattered. And I push him too."

As the two most junior firefighters on Ladder 10, Caouette and Shawn Modahl are usually put in charge of going up on the roof to cut holes for ventilation, and both are eager to be the one who gets the work. Before they arrive at a working fire scene, they play a quick rock, paper, scissors game, with the winner earning the honor of heading up the ladder first. But one night Modahl was experiencing pain in his side and generally not feeling well, so he told Caouette that if their truck got any work that night, it was hers. It was another sign to Caouette that her own crew has the utmost confidence in her ability to do the job.

"He knew I could carry the weight," Caouette says. "I pride

myself on trying very hard to do my job and doing everything that these guys can do. And what really gives me a lot of faith is that these guys have the faith in me that I can do everything they can do. My crew probably has more faith in me than I do. They really support me a lot."

The air is much cooler and far less saturated than it has been in recent weeks, making for a gorgeous late-summer Sunday. The morning has passed relatively quietly — just a few minor medical runs. With their chores behind them, the firefighters await the next call. Some are playing a word game on the computer, while others sit in the dining room reading the paper, conversing, and listening to other companies responding to calls over the radio — some of the downtown crews are performing a water rescue on the Mississippi River.

Shortly after lunch, the bell rings and the electric tones echo through the station for a medical run. Engine 14 is sent out to a house on 31st Avenue on a personal injury run. Captain Kris Lemon is riding in charge today. A seven-and-a-half year veteran with the department, Lemon is small but fit, and beneath her shortly cropped reddish brown hair, her face projects a confident sense of authority. She takes this job seriously and soaks up all she can about the science of fire, rescue techniques, and other technical aspects of the job through reading and extra training. She is known around the department as a captain who is stern and disciplined in the station and on the scene.

Jay Wells is driving and firefighter Laura Pawlacyk is in the rear of the cab as Engine 14 screams through the streets. Pawlacyk is a cheerful and athletic rookie, and her fellow firefighters have already determined her to be compassionate and competent when dealing with victims on medical scenes.

The police have just arrived on the scene as Wells brings the fire engine up to the house on 31st. Lemon and Pawlacyk pull their latex gloves on, grab their medical kits, and stroll calmly up to the house. There are a number of people, mostly women, on the porch, and a baby is screaming. The firefighters sidestep an ice cream bar that is melting in the sun on the short, gray, concrete walkway leading from the sidewalk to the porch. It appears to have only been barely nibbled before being dropped, probably in a panic, and it is softening into a white, gooey mess.

Lemon and Pawlacyk step up onto the porch and immediately go to work assisting a slim, young Hispanic woman who is sitting on a chair. She is sobbing, tear tracks evident on her light cocoa-colored cheeks. In her arms she holds a small baby boy with a tall shock of wavy black hair. The baby is crying with every ounce of energy his tiny lungs can muster. The slim woman seems to be his mother, and she has his hand wrapped in a dishtowel. His pudgy arm and little button-up shirt are covered in blood, which has also spilled onto the woman's white shirt as she clutches him tightly. There are a handful of other women on the porch, three of them black, the others Hispanic. All have looks of concern on their face, but the black women appear to be a bit angry, as well. They seem somehow unhappy with the baby's mother, and in between looks of concern, they shoot her full of steely glances.

Lemon begins slowly unwrapping the towel from around the injured hand, and the baby — his name is Jorge and he is a year old — somehow finds the energy to scream all the louder. The peeled-back towel reveals that Jorge's right thumb is missing. Only a small, white, bony stub poking through a tiny pinch of red tissue is visible through all the blood. A woman who went inside a moment ago returns with a small plastic bag containing Jorge's tiny thumb. She hands it to Pawlacyk, who wraps it up carefully as Lemon tends to the screeching baby. An ambulance arrives, and the three black women move toward the sidewalk to make room for the paramedics. There they explain to a police officer what has happened.

The yard in front of the house is raised several feet above the sidewalk, and a small retaining wall of drab, gray concrete bricks has been constructed about three feet high along the yard's front face. Just beyond the top of the wall is a chainlink fence that runs across the front of the small yard. But the fence ends a few feet short of the southeast corner of the yard, where a small patch of dirt and rocks slopes down to the sidewalk. The women are pointing out this corner of the yard to the officer. One of the large gray bricks from the retaining wall lies near their feet. Next to it is a gruesome spattering of blood that is being swarmed by flies. It seems the brick gave way and the little baby slipped with it. The women say Jorge's thumb was ripped free in the fall. It was not crushed, so it's doubtful the heavy brick severed it by landing on it. It's possible that the tiny hand was snagged in the fence and the thumb was torn off as the weight of his body fell to the sidewalk. Whatever happened, the result is a small baby with a hand that is potentially disfigured for life.

The women speaking to the police officer are becoming louder and more animated as they vent the source of their irritation with Jorge's mother. The women say they live a few houses down, and it turns out those angry glances on the porches were simply the gut reaction of women who have no sympathy for another woman who allows her own child to wander into harm's way.

"Those babies are left out there by themselves all the time," one of the women tells the cop. "Those babies are in the street all the time."

"There's never any parents home," another one says. "You see 'em locked out of the gate and they can't even get back in. And you can't talk to 'em because most of them don't speak English."

"He's lucky he didn't fall on his head!"

Judging by the simmering anger in their voices, it is probably Jorge's mother who is lucky his injuries weren't worse. As bad as losing a thumb is, a blow to Jorge's small skull would have undoubtedly had a more devastating result on the infant. And the righteous maternal ire that would likely have been drawn out of the women from down the street might have meant bad news for the young mother.

But Jorge's poor mother is suffering enough as it is. She is still crying as Jorge is gently loaded into the waiting ambulance, one paramedic carrying the wrapped-up thumb. The firefighters climb back into their rig and begin the trip back to the station. Lemon commends Pawlacyk for trying to make the situation better immediately by calming the people on the deck. They haven't gone far when a call comes in from dispatch.

"Engine 14, stand by for a run," says the dispatcher.

The firefighters, who had been slumped a bit in their seats, come to attention. The call is for someone who is having trouble breathing, and Wells flips on the lights and sirens. He steers the fire engine west on Lowry, south on Penn, then over to a small brown house on Queen Avenue. A man in his early thirties wearing denim shorts and a white T-shirt is waiting on the small wooden porch, and he beckons the firefighters inside.

The house is cluttered and filled with disheveled furniture. On the living room floor is a cat's litter box and a large rodent cage, sans rodent. Sitting on a table is a tall, octagonal aquarium filled with murky yellow water and three sluggish fish. In the kitchen, where dishes and trash are stacked cupboard high on the counters and dining table, a man named John is sitting on a chair and leaning on a rickety table. Above his head is a tattered, cloth wall-hanging that depicts The Last Supper.

John is forty years old and appears sapped of all but his last reserves of strength. He is not wearing any shoes or socks, and his toes twitch with the pain that wracks his body. His thin arms look as if they were once lean and strong, but the muscles have long since atrophied. There are several women in the house making a fuss over the situation, including a woman who says she is John's girlfriend. She informs Lemon that John has leukemia and his medication has run out. They have been urging him to go to the hospital, but he refuses. Here is a man who is so very obviously sick and suffering, but it is just as clear that he is poor. He likely has very little means with which to pay for the treatments needed to battle the disease that is ravaging his body as he enters middle age. His head is bowed and his arms and shoulders convulse slightly, and a large cross dangles from a chain around his neck as Pawlacyk takes his blood pressure and Lemon checks his pulse and begins trying to find out what exactly is bothering him. He only murmurs in response, and the women swirling through the kitchen and the living room say he is having trouble breathing and in great pain nearly all of the time. He is also trembling, and it is beginning to appear that he is intoxicated. A large vodka bottle sits nearby on a box on the floor. The younger man from the porch is now standing nearby. He is tall and strapping — the very picture of health and a total contrast to John. Tears are streaming quietly down the younger man's cheeks.

Lemon asks John where the pain is the worst. He answers that it is all over his body. That it is in his bones. But he does not want to go to the hospital.

One of the women begins screaming at him: "You're going if I have to drag you! You goin' to the hospital!" The other woman is also getting worked up, and the younger man also urges John to go the hospital. The scene is growing loud in the cramped kitchen, and Lemon and Wells begin trying to calm things down.

"Don't pump him up, don't get him excited," Wells says. "He's already pumped up. Okay?"

Most everyone complies and quiets down, everyone except for one short woman wearing a bright red outfit. She snaps back: "That don't excite him! We care, so we say it. We care! That's why we say it."

Wells levels a stern glance at her, and she finally retreats: "Okay, come on, let's let them work"

Lemon crouches next to John and he puts his hand on her shoulder but doesn't look up. His head dangles limply at the end of his thin neck.

"John, a lot of these people care about you. They obviously care about you and we want to get you some help," Lemon says, trying to convince him to take a ride with the paramedics.

"No, no," John says very politely. "You can go, Miss Lady."

Lemon doesn't go anywhere, though, and she and Wells continue to try to convince him to go to the hospital, that it's for his own good. The scene is becoming more chaotic by the moment as more and more people come in and out and add their raised voices to those that are demanding John go to the hospital. Lemon finally stands and goes to the front door to begin stopping the flow of curious neighbors who are peeking in and entering the house.

"Y'all can go, man. Y'all can go," John mutters gently to Wells amidst all the other noises, his head still hanging low.

"We don't mind staying, bro'," Wells says. "We don't mind at all."

"OK, man." A pause. "Man, I gotta lay down."

He stands slowly and shuffles over a few feet to a couch in front of the TV and slumps down. Wells asks him how bad his pain is, on a scale of one to ten. Right now, John says, it's a ten.

The paramedics arrive and the process of extracting information from John begins all over again. The firefighters tell the paramedics what they know, and John continues to insist he's not going in the ambulance. But, he finally concedes, he'll go to the hospital once his brother gets home and can take him. He just doesn't want to go in an ambulance again.

The firefighters can do no more and are getting ready to leave things in the hands of the paramedics.

"I'm feeling a little better, Miss Lady," John says to Lemon. "I'm sorry we bothered you all. It won't happen again."

"We don't mind coming back if we have to," Wells tells him.

"OK, man," John says, and the firefighters leave.

Scenes such as this one in which warm, crowded houses become crucibles of emotion can quickly unravel in a flash of raw passion, and there are times when fire crews have to consider calling for police assistance if things are getting too out of control. In this case, Wells and Lemon were successful in keeping emotional flare-ups from becoming a major problem.

"The first thing to do is always think safety," Lemon says later. "So there's usually the family that's showing emotion, people that are caring, that are worked up about it. But you have to kind of differentiate if it's emotion or if it's a situation where people are under the influence or potentially hostile, because there's a lot of cultural differences and people emote differently. At that scene, people were just charged. They cared. I could tell right away they wanted the guy to get care. So I just wanted to find a safe place for him to be, and then control the number of people going in and out of the house."

On the way back to the station, Lemon has Wells stop the rig when she spots a pile of empty beer bottles and other trash in the street. She jumps out to remove the mess to a nearby garbage can. They stop again a few houses away from the station. A small gray cat is lying dead in the road, its soft fur fluttering softly in the breeze. Four people are standing on the sidewalk staring at the cat. None of them seems particularly distraught, so it is likely not theirs. Lemon asks Pawlacyk to retrieve a garbage bag from the station, and they remove the cat from the street.

Before long, the tones ring out again for another medical run. Engine 14 flies to Oliver Avenue to assist someone who seems to be having heart troubles. As they pull up to the house, a pear-shaped woman with glasses and long red hair flowing over her shoulders and back is standing near the curb. She is holding her purse and seems a bit frozen by the appearance of the fire engine. The firefighters dismount, and the woman tells them she was having pain and tightness in her chest. She called a nurse, who told her to take an aspirin and call 911. She does not seem to be in any pain at the moment, and Lemon asks the woman to sit with her on the concrete steps leading to the house. The woman explains she was taking an over-the-counter pain medication for a toothache, and she wonders if that had anything to do with it. The paramedics arrive, and while the woman has been quietly cheerful since the firefighters first got there, she is suddenly overcome with emotion. Her head drops and she begins to cry, softly at first, then more uncontrollably. She still does not seem to be in any pain, but is instead simply overawed by her predicament. Lemon remains by her side, a reassuring hand on her shoulder. After she calms down, the woman seems thankful as they help her into the back of the ambulance.

It's back to the station, where Pawlacyk begins preparing dinner. Soon the firefighters are gathered in the dining area and eating fresh corn, seasoned potatoes, and herb-crusted chicken breasts. It is delicious, and the others rave as they wolf it down.

The night begins to stretch quietly toward sunset and it begins to seem as if the firefighters might have a quiet Sunday night ahead of them. But shortly after eight, a fire call comes in for a burning park bench across the street from a house on Irving. Wells steers the rig quickly through the streets to the south. He saves a bit of time on the twisting streets by taking the engine off the road and over a playground and park area near the local Boys and Girls Club. There is no burning bench to be found, however, and Lemon approaches the house on Irving. She asks, but no one at the home seems to know where the call came from. There is a small boy hiding around the corner inside the door, though, and he seems nervous, as any little boy who might have called 911 for fun might be.

As Engine 14 heads back, Lemon spots the family of the little boy who lost his thumb earlier in the day entering their home. Wells circles the block in hopes of being able to talk to the family and see how Jorge is doing. But everyone is inside by the time the fire engine gets back to the house, so they decide to move on. Lemon notes that if doctors had been able to reattach the thumb, Jorge would still have been at the hospital as he began his recovery. The fact that he is home so soon after his terrible fall leads the firefighters to believe that Jorge will likely be growing up with a disfigured hand. The large brick that gave way under Jorge's tiny weight still lays on the sidewalk, casting a hard, dark silhouette in the faded daylight.

The early hours of the night are uneventful. The station is quiet and the firefighters begin heading upstairs to bed one at a time around ten-thirty. Anderson is spreading white sheets over his bed downstairs near the coop — he's got night watch tonight — and notes that, although it's been a quiet day for fires, the shift is only two-thirds over. His words prove prophetic, as he's barely finished preparing his sleeping space when the tones ring out evenly for a fire run.

"I knew it," he says as he moves off to pull on his boots near Ladder 10. Lemon and the other firefighters who were already upstairs come spilling down the pole and head to the rigs. Dispatch calls out the address, a house on 25th Avenue. The initial assignment will be Engine 14 and Ladder 10 and another engine company. Engine 14 pulls out first and Wells revs it south on James. As it disappears around the corner, the doors in front of Ladder 10 are opening, and the big truck slips out into the night.

As Wells navigates Engine 14 toward the scene, another call from dispatch comes in saying additional information has been called in by local residents. Fire is plainly visible from outside the house, so dispatch bumps the fire to a first alarm and calls for another two engines, another ladder, and Rescue 1. As Engine 14 arrives at the address, an undulating fork of orange flame can be seen jutting out from a back corner of the house. Lemon radios dispatch that flames are visible, and the firefighters hop out to the street to go to work. Ladder 10's sirens and booming airhorn can be heard close behind.

Wells quicksteps around the engine, pulling hose from the rear bed and revving up the pump. Pawlacyk makes a last-minute check of her equipment, grabs the hose and follows after Lemon, who has disappeared through the front gate and into the overgrown foliage that obscures the front of the abandoned house. As Wells gets the pump up to full pressure, the sirens from the incoming units can be heard screaming toward the scene from all directions.

With axes, hooks, and Halligan tools in hand, Tim Baynard, Elondo Wright, Modahl, and Anderson follow the engine crew through the bushes and pick their way through the darkness to the back of the house, where Lemon and Pawlacyk have found the fire. The plywood that once sealed the rear porch door shut has been torn away and is lying on the grass. The door is burning, the flames attempting to find their way through the porch to the body of the house. Before it can get any further, Wells charges the line and the inch-and-three-quarter hose snaps full of high-pressure water, which Pawlacyk unleashes into the face of the flames. The pressure is unsteady, however, and Wells sees the hose shudder on the pavement in front of the house. He quickly goes to work troubleshooting on his instrument and gauge panel. The pressure is indeed fluctuating, and the big diesel engine growls hard and at a high pitch. The water flow is enough to knock the flames back, but Wells and Battalion Chief Jean Kidd, who has recently arrived, try to determine what's causing the problem with the water flow.

A member of the crew from Ladder 4, which has arrived and set up shop down the street, is swinging an axe at the branches and thick brush that chokes the front walkway, clearing a more accessible path for the firefighters who are trying to get to the rear of the house. Engine 4 is also on the scene and is running a supply line from the hydrant down the street to hook into Engine 14.

At the back of the house, Pawlacyk works the nozzle over the door and porch and the flames are drowned. The ladder crews head in, poking several holes in the walls and ceiling to make sure the fire hasn't made its way inside to hide in the house's skeleton. Other truckies move through the house searching for people. There is no furniture in the house, but someone has clearly been living here. Bags filled with trash are piled in various corners of the empty living room and are strewn through the kitchen. Empty soup cans clutter the kitchen counters. It appears that people, or perhaps an animal or two, have also urinated directly on the floors and walls. Here and there in the vacant rooms a rug or mattress lies on the floor. To the firefighters, this is a sign that prostitutes may have been using the house to conduct business within its concealing walls.

"There are houses like this all over the North Side," one firefighter says. "Whores get in there and do their tricks, then leave."

Whoever was here, the fire looks like no accident. Wooden porch doors usually do not catch fire by themselves, and the door leading from the porch to the interior of the house was left slightly ajar with a refrigerator propped up against it from the inside. If someone started this fire, they apparently wanted to make it tough for the firefighters to get in and do their job. The open inner door also provided an opening into the walls of the second floor, which would have given the flames a largely unhindered path throughout the house's skin. Had a neighbor not spotted the flames so early on and called 911, the house might have burned to the ground.

As the mopping up continues, Wells and Kidd try to find the problem with the ailing pump. Engine 14 is using a spare rig today. The "real" Engine 14 is in the shop receiving transmission repairs, and today the company has been riding an older spare usually housed at Station 16. Aging rigs and dwindling resources make things more and more difficult for everyone from firefighters like Wells to chiefs like Kidd who have to run the show on the scene. Kidd — one of two female battalion chiefs on the department — and Wells are unable to find the problem. So Kidd instructs Engine 14 to switch out this replacement rig for another one at Station 4, which they do shortly after finishing their duties on the fire scene. This second stand-in fire engine is even older than the first, but it will have to do until Engine 14's usual rig is back in working order.

Having to spend so much time shifting their gear from rig to rig the last few days is frustrating to the firefighters. They suffer it with good humor, but they would really like to see an influx of new apparatus to replace the department's aging rigs and spares. Chief Forté hopes to continue replenishing the department's fleet with new rigs, but time will tell if the city and state provide him with the appropriate funding. A handful of new engines were purchased in the late '90s, but many of the regular in-service apparatus date back to the 1980s. The ladder fleet is significantly younger, but the work load of several of the newer trucks could increase before long, as two ladder companies might be put out of service soon, perhaps permanently, to keep up with budget cuts at city hall. Another ladder company is going to be replaced soon by a second heavy rescue unit. Losing those ladders could leave certain parts of the city slightly more vulnerable, as it will take further-out ladder companies longer to arrive after the initial fire alarm. This prospect is particularly galling to firefighters who live with their families in parts of the city that might have a thinner umbrella of resources available, should their own homes ever catch fire.

It is the age-old struggle. While metro fire departments fight tooth and nail to keep the eternal menace that is fire from ravaging the sprawling, aging urban areas they serve, politicians at city hall cut and trim away at the budgets of such core services as fire, police, and rescue. Firefighters especially resent what seems to be the ever-swelling bureaucracy in civic government, which only drains money away from the department and other front-line city entities.

"They have so much money to hand out," says one firefighter, sarcasm dripping from every word, "that I guess they have to pay more people to hand it out."

Budget cuts, it seems, will forever be the bane of crucial city services like the fire department, especially as long as politicians are able to soothe their own consciences when it comes to milking funds away from vital services by applying them to their own pet social projects, which rarely come on the cheap. Firefighters will continue to simmer over the very idea of it, but they will also suffer the cutbacks quietly, for the most part, and do their job, trusting that their own administrators downtown are doing all they can to keep them well-equipped, well-staffed, and well-funded. But there is no denying that aging equipment and thinner resources make for more inherently dangerous fire and rescue scenes for all involved. One can only hope that it doesn't take a death to make those who control the money want to alleviate the strain.

ANSWERING THE BELL

The boy with the blue backpack is watching with great curiosity from across the street. He stands unmoving, a calm center in the middle of a boisterous band of children waiting at the corner for their school buses to pick them up. They are bubbling with laughter and blissfully unaware of the scene unfolding nearby. But not the boy with the blue backpack. Finally, his curiosity becomes too much and he takes one slow step off the curb, then strolls casually but cautiously to the other side of the street. The backpack he wears looks new — school only started a week ago — a shiny metallic blue, but it pales in comparison to the pure, sapphire sky on this dazzling morning. The air is as still as glass, and the bright, clear sunlight illuminates the fresh, green leaves of the massive, burgeoning trees that run up and down the streets around Station 14.

He tries to walk lightly in his big white sneakers so that his footfalls do not disturb the somber ritual that has piqued his interest. Five firefighters are standing at military attention along the edge of the fire station driveway and facing the flagpole some twenty feet in front of them. Laura Pawlacyk is at the base of the pole, her position there befitting her status as the most junior firefighter on today's shift. The air is so still that the flag can barely be seen as it clings limply to the pole at half-mast. Captains Cherie Penn and Tim Baynard are quietly scanning a clipboard that holds the official order of events for the ceremony that is about to begin. The boy has made it to their side of the street. His boldness ratchets up a notch when he realizes that no one has looked in his direction. No one has shooed him away or reacted as if his presence is a distraction. One of the firefighters even turns and looks in his direction, and smiles. He smiles back and, with a sense of wonder shining in his young eyes, strolls quietly up to the end of the short row of firefighters. In perfect imitation, he clasps his hands behind his back and snaps to attention beside them. His only flaw is that his head is cocked up at an angle, looking at the giants beside him in admiration. He quickly realizes that their eyes are pointing deliberately and straight ahead, and he makes the necessary forward adjustments to his own gaze. Five firefighters and an enthralled little boy now stand as one and face the American flag. It is a simple but touching signal of the community's bond with its local firehouse. And it will end up being only the first of many such gestures this 11th day of September, 2002.

It is eerie how this perfect morning so precisely mirrors the weather on this date exactly one year ago. It is the first anniversary of the attacks on America by Islamic terrorists, a day that began clear and beautiful in New York, Pennsylvania, and Washington, D.C., only to be abruptly smudged and smeared with the black smoke of death and destruction. The country is remembering the deaths of thousands of their own, but there is a distinct sense of unease about the whole thing. The actual, horrific events of that day are still too near, too freshly cauterized to regard them as some historic moment to reflect upon. The new kind of war touched off that day is just beginning to unfold, and while the country remembers, it is also reminding itself that there will almost certainly be more mayhem to behold before it is all over, if it ever is.

Death and destruction have always been a part of the firefighter's life, but never quite as terribly as on September 11, 2001, when three-hundred and forty-three of New York's bravest perished in the collapse of the World Trade Center towers — the single greatest firefighter holocaust in history. The Minneapolis firefighters at Station 14 this morning have gathered to reflect on that infamous day when their brothers a good thousand miles away fell in battle. But just as the remembrance is about to begin, Station 14's bell trills loudly, tearing through the stillness. The dispatcher's voice calmly announces that a car has overturned on Penn Avenue, and Engine 14 is to respond. There is no need for any formal order to break rank. Three of the firefighters and Captain Penn simply turn and move toward their rig, which has already been pulled into the open air for the ceremony. Their instantaneous response is perhaps the greatest tribute they could ever make to their fallen comrades from New York. Firefighters know that nothing — nothing — takes precedence over doing their job when called. Their own priorities are set aside the moment the bells go off.

As the engine pulls onto 33rd and heads west, its sirens carving through the clear air, Baynard dismisses the ladder company for a few minutes while he waits to hear through the radio what Engine 14 is facing, and if it will be expected back anytime soon. The three remaining firefighters — Julie Caouette, Mark Anderson, and Shawn Modahl — loll back into the open firehouse while Baynard moves toward the truck, which sits outdoors and has drawn the attention of the boy with the blue backpack. His name is Donnell and he lives down the block. He is ten, although big for ten, with a cherubic face and clear, joyful eyes. He is inquisitive, bright, and clear-spoken, and he puts these gifts to good use by peppering Baynard with questions.

"What do you use that axe for?"

"We use it to cut through things to get to the fire. Through doors. Through walls."

Donnell's eyes widen a bit with surprise.

"You guys cut through walls?"

"Yes, we do."

The inquiry continues, and Baynard is barely finished with each of his answers before Donnell skips on to the next question.

"What do you guys do if a bridge collapses? What would you do if the station was on fire? What would you do if the truck was on fire? What are these poles with hooks for? Why are some of the poles longer than the others? What's this giant fan for?"

Baynard answers all of Donnell's questions and, satisfied with his new store of knowledge, Donnell turns his attention back to the flagpole and asks the fire captain what exactly it was that they were doing over there a minute ago.

"That was a ceremony for September 11. Do you remember what happened last year?"

"Oh yeah, out in California."

"No, in New York and Washington."

A pause.

"Oh yeah, the Pentagon, right?"

"That's right."

Donnell pauses as he continues to gaze at the flag.

"I can't figure out why someone would do something like that," he says softly and looks at Baynard.

"None of us can," Baynard replies quietly.

Penn's voice can be heard over the station radio saying that Engine 14 has arrived on the scene and, although there is no fire showing on the overturned vehicle, they are laying a precautionary line and standing by. Baynard realizes they will be at it for a while, so he calls the remaining firefighters back to the flagpole to resume the remembrance. Anderson and Modahl return to attention, while Caouette has replaced Pawlacyk at the flagpole. Following Baynard's direction, she raises the flag to the top of the pole and they stand at attention for another five minutes, then observe an additional minute of silence as the flag is lowered back to half-mast. People in vehicles rolling slowly through the four-way stop on the corner of James and 33rd peer with sympathetic and admiring eyes toward the small band of navy blue-clad firefighters.

Baynard announces that he is now going to read the names of the New York firefighters who perished in the World Trade Center collapse. Each of the names will be forever remembered as one small flicker of light in what was otherwise a dark and evil day.

Baynard begins: "Adam David Rand...Alan David Feinberg...Allan..."

Three-hundred and forty-three names. It takes nearly ten minutes to read them all aloud. The Minneapolis firefighters listen quietly, knowing that it could have been them, that it would have been them, had the terrorists chosen their city as a target. But there are so very many names, many of them of Irish or Italian descent, that it becomes wearying to hear them all. Three-hundred and forty-three names. That would have been almost our entire department, Anderson thinks to himself.

Baynard concludes with a reading of the Firefighter's Prayer and a moment of recognition for Minneapolis police officer Melissa Schmidt and Esko, Minnesota firefighter Kim Granholm, who were killed in the line of duty in recent months. It is now nine-twenty, and Baynard orders the firefighters to remain at rest until twenty-eight after nine, when they will remember the collapse of the second tower. The buses have picked up most of the kids waiting across the street, and curious motorists continue to trickle by and stare.

Seven minutes pass with the firefighters remaining mostly still and quiet. Baynard checks his watch and is about to move on to the next stage of the ceremony when the station's bell rings again. Just as the Engine 14 crew did before them, the truckies simply turn and move quickly to their rig. The ceremonial remembrance of their fallen brethren will not be completed now, but perhaps that is appropriate, as the firefighter's job is never finished. The future is always open-ended. Emergencies will continue to unfold. Several more minutes of silent observance would no doubt have been appreciated, but firefighters are more at home amidst the clanging, controlled chaos of an emergency run, and these Minneapolis firefighters will pay their homage by doing their duty.

September 11 unleashed one of the greatest series of perspective shifts the country has ever experienced. People began re-evaluating their priorities and what they valued in life and in those around them. Millions of Americans were confronted with their own mortality at that moment when the nation's veneer of invincibility was punctured. Many finally began the journey, off-put for far too long, down the path of personal reflection. And they set aside ample time to ponder the sacrifices made by rescue personnel who stare death in the eye every day. More often than not, firefighters win the showdown, employing their expert training and personal altruism to secure a positive outcome. But there are times when fire carries the day, and death snatches a victim.

Fire is a vicious destroyer. There are few earthly substances it cannot devour. The age-old triumvirate of oxygen, heat, and fuel is all that is required for a fire to spring to life. A number of factors have to line up for enough heat and oxygen to be present for a fire to start, but when it happens, just about anything will suffice as fuel. Wood, of course, is one of fire's favorite delicacies, making wood-constructed homes and buildings and their pocket-filled walls a favorite playground for what firefighters refer to interchangeably as "the beast," "the red devil," and any other of a host of malevolent nicknames. While Hollywood depicts fire as a foe that fights fairly and meets its human challengers right out in the open, the reality is that fire is often difficult to find. It will hide out in walls or ceilings, refusing to expose itself unless the firefighters are clever enough to track it down. And even when fire has found its way out into the open, the smoke is usually so heavy that firefighters can't see their own hand when pressed to the front of their air mask.

"Fire's pretty impressive," says Captain Kris Lemon. "It has its own energy and life. You're afraid of it, but at the same time intrigued by it. It's very powerful and has a mind of its own. It looks for holes and crawls around and can hide from you. So you can be looking for a fire that you know is in a room or on a floor, and you know it's hot, but it's missing one component, which is air. So as soon as you break a window and give it some fuel, it'll show itself. You know it's there, it's just waiting. It just needs enough air to get it going so you can see it."

Finding the fire is always the first priority when firefighters from an engine company arrive on the scene. While the rest of the crew begins readying the pump and hose for the impending battle, the captain of the first-in engine will immediately head into a fire to try and find its point of origin, and assess how far and fast it is spreading. This usually includes a deliberate walk around the structure to ascertain the best points of entry and possible escape routes, followed by a foray into the structure itself to seek the flames. A fire that has been burning for even a short period of time may have cloaked itself in a thick mantle of black smoke, making the captain's job more difficult. But by taking certain visual cues — heavy smoke from a chimney usually means a basement fire, for instance — and paying attention to heat patterns inside, the captain can usually make a well-informed decision on where to look first. This first step is crucial to helping the arriving companies go about their duty. The captain's efficiency is critical.

"Every fire is different," Lemon says. "When I go into a fire, I really am looking at different things. Initially I might go, 'Oh wow, we've got a lot of fire here,' but I'm looking more at where it's at, where it's going, what time of day it is, what I need to do first, where I'm going to lay my line if I'm on an engine, if there's anyone hanging out a window. If I'm on a truck company, I'm going to try and make the best decision about ventilation, how can I help my crew inside, do I need to get on a roof and put a hole in it? All those things race through your head. The only time you really get to stop and take in a fire is when you're standing inside waiting for the water to come."

While the captain is performing reconnaissance, the other members of the engine company are preparing the first-attack hose line and stretching it to the entry point that the captain determines is best. The first salvo of water will flow from the engine's own onboard water tank, while the second-in engine connects one hose to a nearby hydrant, and another into the first engine's pump. As the first engine's crew opens up with water, the first-in ladder crew assists them in search and rescue. The ladder crew also begins ventilating the building by breaking windows and cutting holes in the roof to release smoke, heat, and gases from the fire that, if they themselves ignite, or "roll over," can allow the blaze to quickly spread to multiple places in the structure and get out of control.

The first punch in any firefighting bout is almost always delivered via the nozzle on the end of the first hose line. Finding the fire and knocking it down with water is the top priority once the scene has been made as safe as possible. But getting the nozzle to the flame is not as simple as it might seem. Once the firefighters enter the building with the line, they often cannot see through the smoke, and the firefighters' mental fight becomes as demanding as the physical. At that first moment when all light is blotted out, firefighters sometimes feel a fleeting sense of detachment from their senses, as if they have stepped into a black, nerveless void.

"You go inside, and it's dark, and you don't feel the wall," says Elondo Wright, "and for just a split second you're like, 'Whoa.' You know you're not going to die, you're just scared for a second. But you keep going anyway."

Aside from the captain's initial incursion, firefighters always try to perform their duties at a fire in pairs, and when it is too dark to see, they often try to maintain constant physical contact with each other when moving to avoid getting separated. Smoke can be so dark that the fire itself can only be seen as a dirty glow, if at all. Even when walking or crawling at a slow pace, if firefighters lose tactile connection with each other, they can suddenly find themselves on their own and in great peril. Because of this very real possibility, the third-in engine company is always designated as the rapid-intervention team — the RIT. Engine 14 and Ladder 10 were both second in at a two-alarm house fire a week before today's September 11 anniversary, and the first-in engine company's captain became separated from his rookie firefighter as they crawled through the dense smoke of a fire that was burning its way through a house filled with furniture and waist-high piles of garbage. Another ladder company found the rookie before the RIT was even sent in, but he suffered second-degree burns on much of his upper body before being rescued, earning him a trip to the hospital. The lost firefighter, combined with a poorly selected initial entry point, heavy smoke, and an intense lightning storm outside that affected radio communication, made for a scene that rapidly deteriorated. The crews had to regroup. But it's for precisely these combinations of frenetic circumstances that firefighters train so hard, and their training often triggers the correct responses to pull them through.

"A huge factor is experience and staying calm," says Lemon, who was captain on Engine 14 that night. "If you can picture yourself in a dark environment and you're doing something that's already crazy, and it's hot, you're looking for somebody, trying to follow all these firefighting tactics, and then something happens to your partner or yourself, the number one thing you need to do is stay calm and make good decisions."

Most of the time, though, the firefighters are able to find their way to the flames without any major incidents. And at times when the structure is fully involved and the flames are out in the open, it can be a dazzling display that impresses even the most veteran firefighter. Tom Rogalski was a new captain when he arrived in charge of Engine 14 at a house fire in the summer of 1996. The two-story A-frame was going like a bomb, and had even spread into the front lawn by the time the first companies went into action.

"It was just a giant fireball," Rogalski says. "It was the day after the Fourth of July. It was in the middle of the day and I couldn't figure out how something could get going this good before anyone saw it and called it in. When I opened the door of the rig to get out, the radiant heat from this thing was so hot that I instantly had to turn around to protect my face. It was just so hot."

It turned out that someone had hurled a Molotov cocktail or two in through the front of the house, and the ensuing blaze swept through the wooden structure with an unchecked fury. Once they overcame their initial shock, Rogalski and firefighter Tom Fellegy pulled a tank line to the side of the house and went to work battling the fire. They had fought their way into the kitchen when their line died, and they suddenly found themselves in the middle of a burning room with no water. Backing out quickly, they found the reason for the instantaneous and total pressure drop — the fire on the lawn had munched right through their hose.

But while flames shooting from every window can make for dramatic viewing, perhaps the most awe-inspiring sight firefighters see occurs when gases that have pooled at the top of a room ignite and the flames roll and play across the ceiling like the surface of some churning, hellish sea.

"When you do see fire and see it rolling in the house, it's awesome," says Caouette. "You can see a picture of it on TV or whatever and see what it looks like, but it's a lot different when it's the whole ceiling above your head and it's in 3-D. For most people, it's like getting to see a beautiful mountain scene on a postcard but never experiencing the real thing."

Most firefighters recall the first time they experienced the sur-real effect of flames dancing hauntingly above their head as if it were yesterday. And, even though it is their sworn enemy, they freely admit that it is one of the most beautiful things they have ever seen. Wright remembers his first such encounter well. It was a duplex on Lake Street that had been deliberately set aflame by a young boy.

"The whole room was engulfed and the flames were rolling just like in the movies, and it was so amazing I almost didn't want to put it out," Wright recalls. "And it was so big that I had to get my breath back and start breathing. It was just amazing what I was seeing, and it was breath-taking that I'm in here and I'm con-trolling the water that's trying to knock down this fire. So it's a combination of a lot of things when you get in a big fire, but the main thing you think about is that the people expect you to do the job and they depend on you. I like that part of it."

Most of the time when a fire pulls itself up to the ceiling, it also takes a good deal of the heat with it, which provides an open win-dow of opportunity for firefighters to make a search of the room. But when the fire is located closer to floor level, the heat it can generate can be a shock to the human system, even for seasoned firefighters in their flame-resistant gear. Firefighters often crawl to the fire, not only to get below the smoke, but also to stay beneath the superheated layers of air that become more deadly the closer you move toward the ceiling. Blasting fire with water is effective in most cases because it knocks out two of the three legs — oxygen and heat — that fire stands upon. Going after the fire quickly after they have found the seat of it is also critical to firefighters' ability to remain unshaken by the heat.

"When you get in close, your skin feels like it's going to burn," Caouette says. "When you see flames and it's that hot, you need to open up the nozzle to cool it down and extinguish as much as you can at the time. You can't wait, because in that split second that you wait, you get so hot you can get scared and hesitate."

Of course, just getting water on the fire doesn't do the trick all by itself. If the ladder companies haven't gotten the structure ventilated, the water just turns into trapped steam, and the heat can swell and become even more dangerous. And there are other times when the fire and its heat are not so evident. When fire gets into the walls and lays low while waiting for a breath of air, firefighters often have to try and find it by opening holes in the walls and ceiling to flush it out. Sometimes there is smoke present to give the firefighters a clue where to begin their search, but not always. Most firefighters can recall fires in which there was very little physical evidence that a fire was actually burning somewhere, only to find an entire floor engulfed once a hole in the ceiling on the level below was opened up. Caouette remembers one instance during a stint at Station 16 in which an entire family vacated its home in the middle of the night and called 911 because its smoke detector was sounding. The family exited the house and, seeing no signs of fire, was slightly embarrassed about the whole situation by the time the fire engines arrived on the scene. But Caouette and the other firefighters noticed some smoke seeping from the top of the house and began their search. They could find nothing initially. Then a ladder crew opened up a hole in the ceiling on an upper floor and revealed that the entire rafter structure in the attic was stuffed with flames. The fire was knocked down, and most of the house, not to mention the family, was saved — all thanks to a smoke alarm.

"They all could have died," Caouette says, shaking her head slightly at the thought of what could have been were it not for a small, battery-operated sentinel that so many people neglect to keep operational in their own homes. "The whole family was alive because of one smoke detector that they didn't take apart because they were cooking and set it off, or the battery ran out and they didn't put a new one in."

Still, there are times when even early detection is not enough to avoid massive property loss. Minneapolis assessed nearly thirteen million dollars in fire damage in 2001, but behind the statistics are the real-life losses suffered by citizens whose property is ravaged by fire. Firefighters find few sights as humbling or heartrending as that of a family standing on the sidewalk, watching its possessions burn.

Engine 14 and Ladder 10 recently responded to a three-story apartment fire that went to two alarms at around six-thirty in the morning. It took the fire department three hours of hard work to extinguish the blaze, which spread through the old structure's walls with astonishing quickness. Many of the firefighters went through multiple oxygen bottles, and there seemed to be fire everywhere as they opened the walls and ceilings. They had to tear apart the whole building to make sure they found all of it. In some instances they had to chop through entire walls to get to fire on the other side. As they were mopping up, Caouette felt her heart break a little at all the water that was sloshing in the carpet beneath her feet. Entire apartments were destroyed, kitchens were torn apart, furniture was damaged by smoke or water. Many of the people on the street outside were Hispanic and spoke little or no English. Now, what few possessions many of them had were gone.

"It was sad, just sad to see all those people and trying to think what it was like for them now," Caouette said. "They weren't going to be able to go back in there right away. What were people going to do to explain this at their jobs? And getting clothes, diapers for their kids, daycare, money. There are so many things. It's times like these when it doesn't even feel like you're helping, because the trauma is still so fresh."

Because of its awesome destructive power, fire is even frightening to many firefighters. Indeed, some of them are deathly afraid of the stuff, and most would admit that at least a little fear at any fire scene helps them remain alert and take the right approach to their work. There are not many people who can appreciate the deadliness of fire like a firefighter can.

There are usually a handful of fire-related deaths in Minneapolis every year. In those cases, death often comes at the choking hands of smoke inhalation, with the body already snuffed of life well before the flames actually reach it. Firefighters simply must learn to cope with death on the job, and they are usually able to do so by mentally and emotionally counterbalancing the tragedies with all of the positive outcomes they help bring about. But the sight — and the smell ("You never forget it," Wright says) — of a burned human corpse is arguably the most surreal and sickening experience a firefighter will ever have to deal with. Wright remembers the first fire victim he witnessed — an eight-year-old-boy who became trapped in a house fire and was found badly burnt and hunched over his bed after the fire was out.

"He looked like he was praying," Wright said.

People who have been burned badly in a fire often appear inhuman. The skin becomes tight and waxy, burned smooth and hairless. Rogalski recalls a fire at a loading dock in downtown Minneapolis that killed a homeless man as he slept on a couch on the dock. After the fire was put out, Rogalski asked a rookie who was with him if he had seen the dead man at the bottom of the steps.

"That wasn't a real person," came the rookie's incredulous reply.

Rogalski assured him that it was, but the rookie remained unconvinced — until, that is, he was able to make a face-to-face inspection of the corpse.

The man's coat sleeves had burned away, and Rogalski remembers wondering if the police would be able to tell what time the man died by looking at the watch that had stopped and was still strapped to his wrist.

Being trapped and killed by fire is one of the human race's greatest fears. Yet even after watching people jump hundreds of stories to their certain deaths live on television on September 11, most still have a hard time fathoming what it must be like to have an incinerating entity whirling towards you and cutting off your only hopes of survival. The desperation that sweeps over the human soul at such a moment must be more atrocious, more overriding, than we can ever imagine. And firefighters see people do astonishingly illogical things when threatened by fire. Some firefighters in Minneapolis have witnessed people become overwhelmed by panic when they are in a burning building, even if they are not in any real danger at the moment. Often they feel compelled to jump, fully accepting the dire, and potentially deadly, consequences that might result from their leap. Somewhere in the human psyche lurks a trigger that chooses this desperate option over being burned alive.

"I think the worst thing about fire is just watching people panic," Lemon says. "It's pretty horrible to know that there's a fire in an apartment building and people are jumping from the third floor because they don't know what else to do. People have seen that on TV now, but there's something completely different about seeing it in real life. These are people's homes and they're scared and they jump out a window when, really, they were safe. But you can't control people's fear when you can't get to them."

And firefighters must often overcome their own reflexive fears in order to spring into action when people are trapped by fire. It might mean going into a dangerous fire more aggressively than they would otherwise, or it could mean climbing a hundred feet of ladder propped on the roof on a cold and windy night to rescue someone who is blocked off from all other escape routes. Again, these are moments when training takes over and firefighters just act.

"You just have to put those fears aside," Caouette says.

Says Lemon: "It's just what we do. I think everybody works very hard to do the best job they can. There's something very humbling about a fire scene. People just want to do what's right, so they listen and they work together."

Rogalski has seen a lot in his decade and a half on the job, but no fire-related death affects him as much as that of a baby he could hear screaming on the other side of a door in a burning duplex.

"We were on the landing and pulling our masks on and trying to get in there, and it was just this screaming baby, man," Rogalski says. "I've never heard anything like that scream."

The firefighters finally burst through the door and found the room filled with flame, smoke, and intense heat. They could no longer hear the baby and, after knocking the flames down, they found the tiny child on the floor, dead. It is the one incident in his career that Rogalski says he still has trouble talking about.

"That poor baby," Rogalski says quietly. "It was bad."

But when a firefighter in Minneapolis experiences death on

the job, more often than not it occurs on a medical run. Whether it's high-trauma car crashes, stabbings and shootings, or simply death from natural causes such as heart attacks or other medical conditions, firefighters see it all. Often they are the first person to determine that a victim is dead, or even the last human being the person sees or speaks to before they die. Wright's first non-fire death was a woman in her fifties who seemed to be choking.

"I remember we went in there and they just thought she went unconscious, so we get there and took a pulse, and there was no pulse," he recalls. "Then we tilted her head to check for an obstruction, because we were going to try to put air in and wanted to make sure there was nothing blocking it. I remember my glove going in her mouth and feeling her tongue and knowing she was dead. There's no other feeling like a cold, dead tongue on your fingers."

Wright admits being shaken by this first brush with death, and it took some time for him to come to terms with the fact that a life had ended, and that there was nothing he could do about it. Worse, he had to deal with the mind-bending idea that, although this woman was gone, the world continued to turn.

"We were on our way back to the station past the lake," he says, "and the water was no different, the world was no different, everybody was walking around with ice cream, the trees were still moving the same. The other firefighters were older, so they were still the same. Nobody changed, and I don't know if I expected trumpets to go off when this lady died, but the world was still the same, except there was just one less person."

Through that encounter, coupled with the small boy who died hunched over his bed in a fire, Wright also experienced a conscious recognition that death can take anyone at any moment. It shook a major tenet of the culture around him that worships and sells the image of youth as invincible.

"I realized death has no age limit," Wright says. "It amazes me how we can go one hour and an old person could die, and the next hour we could bring somebody into the world. You always know that people can die, but when you see someone die in front of you, it's a whole new ballgame. It's a whole new ballgame."

In moments when firefighters are called in to help a person who is not yet dead, but very apparently soon will be, they simply try to do the best they can to comfort them emotionally and physically, as well as keep them from being subjected to public spectacle. And whether it's administering pain-relieving first aid or just holding someone's hand, in short, they try to help the person die with dignity.

Rogalski remembers firefighters trying to save a woman who lit her bed aflame — apparently intentionally — while she was lying in it. The woman was still alive even after Rogalski's crew, which was the second-in engine, arrived and had stretched a backup line to the blaze. A ladder company hauled her into the hallway to get her out of the room. She was burnt horribly, and her badly traumatized body gave out shortly thereafter.

"That was fourteen years ago," Rogalski says, "but it was one of those images that just gets burned into your mind."

Rogalski recalls another time when a good buddy of his was on a crew that arrived on a construction site and found a worker who had been accidentally pinned to a wall by the massive, earth-scraping plow of a bulldozer. The thick steel spikes along the edge of the plow had plunged through his midsection and were now all that was keeping the man, who was still alive, from falling into two pieces. The man had reflexively put his hands out to each side to resist the oncoming machine, and one massive spike had gone through each of his palms, as if he had been crucified. He was in shock. Rescuers knew the man would likely die as soon as the equipment was pulled back, and he muttered a few words of love for his wife before finally expiring.

Yet as tragic as it is to witness someone inhale their last breath of air, the reaction of the person's loved ones can be even more distressing, even dangerous, for firefighters. Reactions of people who are informed that a cherished friend or relative has suddenly been snatched away from them can run the entire spectrum — from quiet shock and disbelief to vocal and physical hysteria of such a high degree that firefighters have actually feared for their own safety.

"Death doesn't really bother me now, but the after-effects of seeing family members react to it, to see emotion, to hear a scream or a feeling or a word that is so deep in their heart for someone who dies, that is something that a greeting card can't represent," Wright said. "I saw one lady die and the family came in and broke windows, broke the phone, wanted to fight, the daughter fainted. I thought we would have to call the police."

Firefighters also learn quickly not to try and force any artificial, I-know-just-how-you-feel sentiment on people, because usually it doesn't register with the person hearing it. Instead, they just try to offer a basic sense of human respect and sympathy for the person who has just died, as well as a strong hand to hold for the loved ones left behind.

"You can't say, 'Well, I know what you're going through,' because you don't," Wright says. "Everybody thinks they can say they know what you're going through because they've had someone die, too, but you don't know. You don't know what kind of bond they had, because every situation is unique. So at first I would say, 'I know what you're going through,' but I stopped because I don't want to get a script in life. I want to be sympathetic to a person's needs and say I'm sorry and just be there for that person."

Never has that genuine sympathy flown in the other direction so freely as it did in the immediate aftermath of September 11. After so many died in New York, firefighters across the country were suddenly, for once, on the receiving end of a tidal wave of public support and appreciation. Firehouses in Minneapolis and around the country were showered with flowers, balloons, letters, cookies, cakes, and all other types of appreciative gestures. Many people stopped in just to offer a humble thanks. In the neighborhoods where firefighters live, people made a point of stopping by to express gratitude during their off-duty hours. One of Wright's neighbors came to the door of his home and asked, with a grave expression on his face, if he could speak to him outside. Wright immediately thought maybe his kids had broken the neighbor's window and the man was there to demand retribution.

"But then he stuck out his hand and said, 'I just want to tell you I'm really sorry for your brothers and sisters,'" Wright recalls.

"The way he said it, and I knew this man, and I had never seen such emotion from him. I mean, he knew I was a firefighter and we talked about it, but I don't think he really knew what I did on a daily basis. I think people are looking into our lives more and knowing that we are regular humans trying to save other humans, and doing things that a lot of other people wouldn't do. I think people are starting to appreciate us a lot more, but I'm sorry it took a tragedy to make that happen. And I'm not looking for glory or fame, but I guess I like for people to know that we're putting our life on the line to save them."

On the day marking the first anniversary of the terrorist attacks, people who live around Station 14 trickled in throughout the afternoon hours to show their appreciation. Children and their parents arrived to present the firefighters with muffins and cookies, which the firefighters happily accepted, offering tours of the station in return. One elementary school teacher dropped off dozens of small paper stars decorated by her students with messages of love and support, such as "Firefighters Save The World."

Caouette and Dan Schultz are taping all of the stars to a wall in the coop when Donnell returns with his siblings and his mother and some of their friends. Donnell is carrying a giant rectangular cake with the words "Thank You For All You Do" emblazoned on it with bright orange icing. Caouette and Pawlacyk offer to show them around the station, and Donnell and the other kids begin gleefully climbing on the rigs. Caouette entertains them with stories about station life. The kids — and the women who brought them in — let out a whoop of laughter when Caouette says that you can always tell who snores in the night by the number of toilet paper rolls that lay scattered around their beds in the morning. The other firefighters chuck them toward the source of the noise in the middle of the night, she explains.

Pawlacyk asks Donnell, who is sitting wide-eyed in the captain's seat of Engine 14, how school was today. Fine, he says, they watched an interesting movie about the ocean. But he quickly adds that he doesn't like school and doesn't know if he'll finish. Pawlacyk tells him he'll need to finish school if he wants to become a firefighter someday, and you can almost see the words physically seeping into his brain as he slowly nods and his brow furrows slightly. These simple few words from the mouth of a firefighter might have done more than all the classroom incentives he ever receives to make sure this bright, inner-city youth sees his education through.

Death and destruction will always be part of the firefighter's calling, and they will continue to discover their own individual ways to deal with it, as well as find relief from the constant reminders of their own mortality. For many of them, the release they employ is simply to find a way to enjoy themselves after returning to the station, to keep their spirits up, to laugh.

"You learn how to cope, and thank God firefighters have a good warped, dry sense of humor, because that's a release afterwards," Lemon says. "But sometimes you can't. You're just a person, and you don't want to suppress it so much that you can't feel."

The maelstrom of emotions that death unleashes in the human heart is something most firefighters will have to confront, and eventually harness, sometime during their careers. And while it does make them acutely aware of the thread by which every human life dangles, it also makes them appreciate their own lives, their own friends, their own families, and their own jobs all the more.

"Everybody always says you should give people roses while they can smell them, and that's what it made me start to do," Wright says. "It has made me appreciate and cling to life, because I know how life can be. I feel more love for my kids. When I see them, it's something to be thankful for because, you know, life is what you expect it to be. So I feel more love for the kids. Even just being away from them for twenty-four hours makes me appreciate them more."

This is what keeps firefighters coming back for more. It's what keeps them from hesitating when it's time to run into another burning building to pull someone out.

"That's what we do," Wright says, "and that's what we'll continue to do."

ANSWERING THE BELL

Photos © 2003 Brett Knapp

Brett Knapp

ANSWERING THE BELL

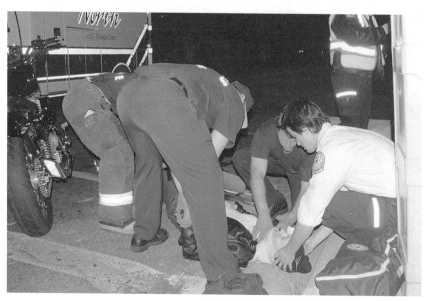

Photos © 2003 Brett Knapp

ANSWERING THE BELL

The riot broke out as the curtain was falling on a heavenly, late-summer Thursday evening in the Jordan neighborhood, about seven blocks from Station 14. Minneapolis police arrived at a house on the North Side to serve a warrant for suspected drug activity. A man in the yard ignored police requests to remove a growling pit bull from the area and instead removed its leash, freeing the dog to attack the officers. One of the cops fired at the dog, killing it. But a bullet ricocheted off the sidewalk, striking an eleven-year-old boy in the arm. Police cordoned off the area, but a crowd soon gathered and rumors began to swirl.

The police had shot a young boy. That sentiment, unencumbered by important details about the dog or the accidental nature of the shooting, threaded through the crowd like Eden's serpent, igniting the pent-up frustrations of the residents in the neighborhood. Two other blacks had been shot by police in Minneapolis in the past year, and even if the police officers had done so in self-defense, the flying bullets served to galvanize tensions between the thin blue line and North Side residents.

The suppressed anger and desperation was boiling to a froth in the crowd, and soon things were getting out of control. Police pulled out as media crews began to arrive. The people in the streets no longer had the police at which to vent their anger, so the reporters would have to do. Journalists from local newspapers and television stations who had come to the scene to objectively scoop up the dramatic details of a police shooting soon found themselves the center of attention. Two reporters from the *Star Tribune* were attacked and beaten, one of them badly. News crews watched helplessly as their vehicles' windows were smashed out. They quickly realized their predicament and tried to flee. But before long, one station's SUV was aflame, and the C-shift crews from Station 14 were called in to extinguish the blaze.

It's been some thirty-six hours since the riot started, and the A crews are reporting for another shift on a sunny Saturday morning. They have not heard many details about the riot from their colleagues who were called into the danger zone Thursday night, but they know enough to be a little extra cautious today. Much of the day and a half following the violence were filled with pleas for peace by city officials and citizens of the neighborhoods involved. But the news media have also quoted some folks as saying that things might just get worse before they get better. One person in the newspaper even openly hinted at the possibility of "another Haaf" taking place, referring to the racially charged murder of Minneapolis police officer Jerry Haaf, who was gunned down in cold blood while sitting at a small pizza shop in south Minneapolis in 1992.

Peace is doing its best to sweep through the neighborhood today, but there are clearly still pockets of hatred that have been too long in the making to be so easily washed away by a couple days of prayers, promises, and calls for goodwill from city and neighborhood leaders.

The firefighters on the North Side probably have little to fear, as their reputation among the citizenry here has been golden for a long time. But one never knows. Logic and reason were snowed under by emotion and rage on the corner of 26th and Emerson on Thursday night, and the firefighters know they might be called into environments where emotion will be the reigning force today. In some cases, the police will also be on hand and working side by side with the fire department, further increasing the possibility

116

that the firefighters could find themselves caught up in a bad situation.

The morning comes and goes with one false fire alarm, and because it is Saturday — cleaning day — the firefighters spent much of it washing down the station and the fire engines. Captain Tom Rogalski and several others are now sitting around the dining room table. Rogalski just looks like a firefighter. He's not as big as some of the others, but he is lean and wiry with a handsome face and a full head of well-groomed dark hair. When riding in charge of Ladder 10, he is laid back but always alert, with his left arm usually slung up on the console between the front seats. Rogalski is half-Irish, half-Polish, and grew up as one of eight kids in a small house in a North Side neighborhood that used to be populated with firefighting families. He graduated from Patrick Henry High School in 1982, and around Thanksgiving of that same year was working in downtown Minneapolis at a yogurt shop owned by his buddy Mike Fust's aunt (Fust, incidentally, is also a firefighter in Minneapolis now). Right down the street from the shop, a few kids playing around in an old, abandoned building ignited an inferno that ended up consuming almost an entire block, including the Norwest bank tower. There was a fire engine parked in front of the yogurt shop when Rogalski came to work in the morning, and he provided the firefighters with free coffee all day long while they relayed water to the wet, chilly fire scene. These days, he keeps a low profile around the firehouse, but he is also one of the station's best storytellers, and he is currently regaling the others with an amazing tale. A few days back, Rogalski had filled in at Station 8 — known within the department as "Crazy 8s" — in South Minneapolis.

"There was this guy banging on the door," Rogalski begins, "and we go out there and there's this cabbie, and he says, 'This guy in the back of my cab is taking all his clothes off.' So we go out there and, sure enough, there's this guy who's completely naked sitting in the back of this cab. He's got this pen and he's writing stuff all over his thighs. And then he takes this shoestring and starts wrapping it around his penis."

That last detail gets everyone in the room's interest. Those who were only half-listening are now paying rapt attention to the captain's story.

"And he takes the string in both of his hands and starts yanking it upward like he's trying to pull it off, ya know? So I start yelling, 'Hey! Hey! Stop that!' But the guy just gets out of the cab and puts the string down between his legs and pulls it up from behind and starts yanking it again."

All the guys in the room are now laughing and squirming at the same time.

"Now, I don't know what this guy is going to do next, so I order everyone back into the station and call the cops. So now we're all standing inside, and the cabbie is inside with us, and we're watching this guy through the windows and he starts walking away down the street. The cops get there and set him down, so we grabbed the medical bags and walked down there. Well, this guy is telling them he was gang-raped by a bunch of guys down on Franklin or something, but the cabbie says he picked him up in Chanhassen, so who knows?"

The others ask if the man seemed to have been beaten up at all or anything and Rogalski says no. The guy just seemed to be having some sort of mental problems. The firefighters just chuckle and shake their heads in disbelief at the man's apparent attempt at self-mutilation. The story reminds Elondo Wright of a time he attended to a man who had been shot in the genitals.

"You know what a hot dog looks like when it splits apart in a microwave?" Wright remarks.

A few minutes before noon, the alarm sounds. Engine 14 is dispatched to a house on Dupont to assist a person who is vomiting blood. Jay Wells fires up the freshly scrubbed fire engine as Wright, who is filling in as captain today, climbs into the other front seat. Leonard Crawford, a second-year firefighter tramping in at Station 14 today, hops into the rear of the cab, and they're off.

The drive is a short one, and as the engine wheels up in front of the house, a thin bespectacled white man with curly brown hair and a mustache waves frantically with one arm. He appears to be in his early thirties, and once he realizes the firefighters have

118

spotted him, he instantly drops his arm and casually lights up a cigarette.

Just inside the door of the house, a shockingly obese man wearing only a pair of shorts and a light blue sling on his arm sits piled into a huge recliner that is straining to contain the man's bulk. He is massive, and the wispy brown beard dripping from his oddly boyish face looks fake somehow. Crawford asks if he's the one having trouble, and the man laughs jovially.

"No," he says, still chuckling. "I just look sick. She's through there."

The house is like so many others in this neighborhood. Dishes and trash litter the kitchen, and what little furniture there is, is old and decrepit. Pictures on the walls hang askew, lending an additional air of chaos and carelessness to the dwelling. The man with the cigarette leads the firefighters to a rear bedroom, and as they turn the corner through the door, they are hit head-on by a sour, biting stench. It is a smell of blood and feces mixed in with stale sweat, and it is overpowering. But the firefighters do not flinch as they move through it to the bed where a small, pale, sweaty woman lies on a mess of sheets and blankets. The light in the room is a dull yellow that seeps in between two oversized beach towels that have been hung as curtains.

Crawford asks for her name and immediately tries to talk to her in loud but calming tones to determine what is ailing her. It becomes clear that the woman, whose name is Lisa, suffers from some sort of neurological debility. She seems almost completely unable to control any of the muscles in her body as she attempts to sit up, and what words she can squeeze out are labored and hard to understand. She seems to be about thirty, and there is a wild look in her blue eyes that makes her appear constantly startled.

Wright and Crawford ask several questions of the man with the cigarette, which is adding its own acrid haze to the already putrid air. The man speaks in a high, nasally voice, and his eyes bulge slightly whenever he talks. Crawford wonders if he has any inkling that the smoke from his cigarette only adds to the unhealthiness of the air in the room, but says nothing. Another woman standing in the doorway says Lisa has multiple sclerosis, but the man with the cigarette interrupts her. No, no, he says, she has ataxia, and beyond that the doctors do not know exactly what is wrong with her. Ataxia is a nasty affliction that impairs one's ability to control their muscles. People who suffer from it long enough can end up completely incapacitated. Another woman enters the room carrying several bottles of prescription medications that Lisa takes regularly. The woman hands them to Wright.

The paramedics come through the door, and the firefighters ask if Lisa is able to walk at all. The answer is no, she needs a walker or a wheelchair. As they slowly sit her up on the bed, her cheeks fill up like a balloon with vomit. The man with the cigarette produces a square plastic dish, and Lisa droops her head inside it and expels several glops of red, mucusy blood. The firefighters carry her the few feet to her wheelchair and set her down gently. As they roll her through the kitchen, Lisa leans over and spits up more blood into the garbage can. She vomits a few more small amounts of blood into the square dish on her way to the ambulance. As the firefighters slowly file out of the house with their medical bags, the overweight man in the chair eyes them with awe. He jokes that if he ever falls down, he'll be sure to call the fire department.

"All of these big, strong guys will be able to help me up," he chortles.

"It'll take every one of y'all to lift him," says one of the women who lives there. "He weighs 420 pounds." The man laughs again. The firefighters bid him a good day and return to their rig.

Just as they begin climbing back into their seats, the on-board call box rings out with another medical alarm. There is a personal-injury incident at the corner of 33rd and Emerson, which is only a block away from their current location. Wells hits the sirens and jams the accelerator, and as the fire engine screams around the corner onto Emerson, several smashed and steaming vehicles can be seen up ahead in the next intersection. About twenty people who have heard the crash are running down the street toward the chaotic scene, and Wright decides this could be more of a situation than the three-man crew can handle, so he radios dispatch and asks for Ladder 10. By the looks of the vehicles involved, the big rig's additional manpower and cutting tools might very well be needed.

The scene is hectic as the fire engine pulls to a stop near the intersection. People are spilling into the streets to get a look at the bashed and steaming remains of an old Pontiac Grand Am that sits in the middle of the road, the accordioned remains of its front end facing the curb. Two other vehicles are also heavily damaged, including a green minivan that has been blasted from behind. The force of the blow has lifted the back of the van up into the air and almost completely off its rear axle. The van has been pushed forward into a light silver Oldsmobile coupe, which has also sustained a good deal of damage.

The firefighters dismount and make their way through the people gathered around and move toward the Pontiac, which is hissing and oozing fluids. A slick of green radiator fluid is forming on the street near the front of the Pontiac, and the hot-baked chemical smell of the stuff is thick in the air. Some other liquid — possibly gasoline — is dribbling from beneath the vehicle's trunk, and Wells moves quickly to sprinkle copious amounts of sand on the fluid to soak it up and keep it from running any further.

Amazingly, despite the devastated condition of the vehicle, the driver is trying frantically to start the engine. But the entire front end is crushed, and the turning of the key serves only to produce an impotent clicking noise from the dead vehicle. Wells sternly instructs the driver — a heavy, grungy man with shoulder-length, stringy blonde hair — to stop trying to start the vehicle as Crawford climbs into the back seat and begins talking to the man, who is in almost as rough a shape as his car. The man is wearing dirty, light blue jeans and a sleeveless, purple T-shirt stretched over a bulbous potbelly. The fact that he apparently does not even realize how badly destroyed his car is, along with his own sluggish movements, lead the firefighters to believe the man is drunk, but that is for the police to say for sure. Their only job is to do their best to begin administering first aid to a very battered human being. The man's forehead is bleeding and his face is red and puffy. A bubbled-out area of the spider-webbed windshield shows where the man's forehead hit it upon impact. Finally realizing that his car will not start, and in obvious pain, the man clutches onto the steering wheel and begins sobbing dryly through clenched yellow teeth, several of which are missing. But his mouth is not particularly bloody, so it looks like they were missing before the accident occurred. His expression is pained, but also a bit fearful as he gazes outside of the car. There is a discernible current of distaste for the driver rippling through the crowd of about three dozen people. Witnesses are describing how the car came careening down the residential street at high speed and slammed into the other two vehicles, which were parked along the curb. Many of the people in the crowd are black. The driver is white. And racial tensions are still taut after Thursday night.

"Mother-fucking drunks," one black woman mutters loudly, but for the most part, there does not appear to be much hostile intent to go with the anger. Still, the man is probably lucky he could not get out of his car with his injuries. If he had tried to flee the scene on foot, there would likely have been plenty of folks to slow him down or physically detain him, perhaps somewhat roughly, until the authorities arrived.

From behind, Crawford is placing a neck brace on the man to stabilize his head as Ladder 10 comes blaring up the street. Several people scatter to make way at the sound of its sirens. Caouette brings the long, flat backboard from the truck. The firefighters will strap the driver to the board once they get him out of the front seat. Crawford has the man's neck braced now, and the firefighters go to work trying to slowly slide him out of the driver's seat. He is in a lot of pain, and he screams out as he grabs his right leg. But the firefighters have to get him out, so they extract him as gingerly as they can, despite his cries.

As he is strapped to the board, another man wearing nothing but sandals and a pair of jean shorts is darting around the scene taking pictures with a small point-and-shoot camera. He lifts the camera above his head at arm's length several times as if he is trying to get several different angles. The green minivan, it turns out, belongs to him. The Oldsmobile is his ex-wife's.

"I was inside watching 'Planet of the Apes' when I heard this kerbloom!" he tells a bystander. "Usually my kids are outside playing right there," as he points to the edge of the yard near the dev-

122

astated van, "but I sent them to their grandmother's this weekend because the neighborhood's been so unsettled."

He shakes his head as he stares at his children's play spot. Had they been outside playing this day, they likely would have been sprayed with the bits of glass and plastic that are lying all around the area.

Another man says he was sitting in the parking lot across the street when he saw the Pontiac run a red light at Emerson and Lowry and broadside a van. The initial collision spun the Pontiac around, and the driver gunned the engine and headed north. But he didn't get very far before careening out of control and into the parked vehicles. The witness says he thinks the man was going about fifty miles per hour through the tight residential streets as he fled after the first impact. It is starting to look as if the driver wanted to avoid being caught at all costs. The Pontiac does not have any license plates, either, leading to speculation that perhaps the vehicle was even stolen. There is also a pair of long-handled bolt-cutters in the backseat. But the inquiries into why the man seemed to be running will be left to the police, who are now on the scene directing traffic and questioning witnesses. The driver has been lifted into the ambulance, and once the firefighters make sure there is no danger of a fire breaking out, their job is done and both crews return to the station.

The engine crew decides to head north to pick up food for lunch at the grocery store. As they pull up to a stop sign, a thin young woman wearing faded pink sweatpants with a cell phone attached to each hip and a white Calvin Klein T-shirt runs up to the driver's side door of the fire engine. Her face is puffy, and she appears to have been crying. Her shirt is abnormally stretched out in two spots, as if someone has been pulling on it.

"He stole my car! He stole my car!" she shrieks over and over. "That guy right there stole my car, and I don't know what he done with it!"

She points to a stocky young man who is walking very calmly down the street in the opposite direction of the fire engine.

"That's my girlfriend from Illinois," the woman continues, pointing to a worried looking woman in a nearby car. "She's my witness. She's not even from here, but she saw it!"

The man finally wheels around and jogs back to the fire engine and shouts: "If I just stole it, would I just be walking right now?"

Wright opens his door and stands on the top step of the rig and attempts to calm the woman down. Wells has already radioed for a squad car, and Wright tells the woman that the police are on their way. As the man resumes his stroll down the street, the woman continues: "He stole it! I just bought that car and he took it. I came after him and he said, 'Bitch, I didn't take it!' and I said, 'Yes, you did!' and he said, 'Bitch, you ain't getting your fucking car back' and shit. Then he pushed me down and started fighting me and started choking me."

The firefighters empathize with the woman, but it is not their job to apprehend criminal suspects. All they can do is take a slow spin around the block and attempt to direct the police via radio. But the man has disappeared before police arrive, so the firefighters roll back to the corner where the woman is standing and inform her that she should wait until the police come. Nothing more they can do, the firefighters continue on their way to get lunch.

Shortly after they return to the station and eat their meals, Engine 14 is called out to another car accident. They fly down the street to Lowry and Sixth and find another green minivan — it's turning into a bad day for green minivans — that has been hit by a red car. Both are smashed up pretty badly. There is no one in the red car now, and a witness says the driver was a pregnant woman who got out of her car and fled the scene on foot. The firefighters ask other bystanders if anyone is hurt and needs help, but no one does. A call comes over the radio that police have found the woman in a nearby apartment building. The officers say she is not injured, so the firefighters are released and head back to the station.

Just after dinner, another call for a personal injury car accident comes in and Engine 14 rolls again, this time to the 3500 block of Lyndale. There is a red sedan sitting right smack in the center of the front lawn of a nearby house. It is well beyond the sidewalk, a good ten yards from the street. It's an odd sight. In the intersection just to the south, a crunched-up yellow Eldorado is steaming and dripping engine coolant. Another large crowd has gathered. Wells and Crawford check the car on the lawn and find an Asian woman in her forties sitting in the driver's seat. She has her eyes tightly closed and one hand over her forehead in an expression of mingled pain and disbelief. The firefighters have to ask her if she is injured several times before she finally answers, but she speaks too quietly for them to hear her. So Wells asks her to point to the pain and she indicates the left side of her face, which does not appear to be cut or bruised in any way. As paramedics and police arrive, and certain that the woman is more shaken up than anything, Wells and Crawford walk over to the yellow vehicle. Wright is talking to a pair of young black men in their late twenties who also appear stunned but not too badly hurt.

The driver of the car is a large man with shiny, thick, black braids dripping out from beneath his baseball cap. He has a slight cut above his eye, and the police invite him into the squad car to tell them what happened. Wells asks the other man if he has any history of medical problems, and he shakes his head no. The man then smiles and says, "Someone hit me in the back of the head with a pipe a while back, though. I just moved here too. Welcome to Minnesota, huh?"

As police continue to sort out what went wrong, the area around the crash begins to take on an almost carnival-like atmosphere as the day fades into twilight. Neighbors drawn out to their front yards by the crash have grown somewhat bored with it and are now talking and laughing with each other. Several small boys are dribbling a basketball and whooping and hollering as they try to snag it from each other. A few young boys on bikes creep up to the yellow vehicle and curiously inspect its smashed-in front end. Crawford spots them and tells them to move away, then begins disconnecting the car's battery with bolt-cutters to keep it from possibly igniting a fire. One of the kids on the bike watches and says to his friends, "Let's get out of here. This shit might blow up." And they ride off down the street.

Wright helps the driver from the squad car to the ambulance, and Wells and Crawford spread sand over the bright green coolant draining toward the curb. One of the police officers bids the firefighters a good night, and as they are driving back to the station, Wells wonders aloud about all the accidents they've seen so far this shift.

"This is going to be a long night," he predicts. "Everyone seems to be in a hurry."

Rather than head directly back to the station, Wells and Wright decide to take the fire engine on a slow cruise around the Jordan neighborhood to get a feel for the mood on the street tonight. Teenagers are beginning to spill onto the street corners. On some nights in the inner city, just as the sun is setting, the streets teem with unusual, almost surreal, visual snapshots. Tonight they seem to be taking place on just about every block. On one corner, an elderly black man with a long, gray beard, dark sunglasses, and a beret perched on his head is crouched next to a chainlink fence. His head is tilted back, and smoke is rising languidly from his lips. A couple of blocks away, a small white boy with dirty brown hair is standing motionless on the porch of an old house. He is shirtless and wears only a pair of dirty brown jeans that are so long that they completely cover his feet, the cuffs dangling over the step in front of him. He stands gazing like a statue out at the street as the fire engine rolls by. Two Mormon missionaries — young, clean-cut white boys with white shirts and black ties — stand amongst a sea of tired black faces at a bus stop. Snapshots of the city.

But as the rig moves from block to block, the firefighters get the sense that local residents are making a concerted effort to get out and enjoy the night together, to restore their neighborhood on this first weekend after the most recent outbreak of violence and discord, to refuse to live up to the poor reputation that people on the outside looking in might try to impose on their corner of the city. Children flock to an ice cream truck at a street corner. Many people are out for a stroll, while others are holding backyard barbecues, where black and white residents are eating, laughing, and sharing their space together. As the fire engine rolls past one such gathering, many of the people in the yard put hamburgers and hot dogs down on paper plates and wave to the firefighters. One woman hurries to the fence and snaps a photo of the rig as it passes down the street. It might not end up being such a long night, after all.

Satisfied with their reconnaissance, the firefighters decide to make their way back to home base. On their way, they pull over to the curb near a convenience store to pick up a few things. As they come to a stop, Crawford calls the others' attention to a car near one of the gas pumps. The car is gushing steam from beneath its hood. Wright radios dispatch about the situation and says they will check it out. As the firefighters approach the hissing car, they notice that there are three small children sitting in the backseat and no adults present. Crawford and Wells move quickly to get the kids out of the car as Wright inspects the front of the vehicle. A young heavyset woman appears through the door of the convenience mart and stops in her tracks in surprise when she sees the firefighters evacuating the children from her vehicle.

"It ain't no fire!" she exclaims as she walks briskly toward the car. "It's just a hose. It ain't no fire!"

"Okay, okay," Wright says, smiling. "Well, we just wanted to make sure it was okay."

The firefighters open the hood and allow the hot steam to dissipate. Now that they've seen for themselves that there is no fire, they relax a bit and Wells peels off to head into the store. The woman who owns the car seems little bit embarrassed, but grateful for the help.

"Where did you come from so fast?" she asks with a big smile.

"We were just over there and saw it, so we had to check it out," Wright says, pointing out the rig.

Several people have now gathered around and are smiling and joking about the situation, completely at ease around the firefighters. Just then, a police car rolls by and all eyes lock on the squad as it moves down the street. The large woman's smile evaporates. Everyone seems to tense for a moment. After Engine 14 begins back toward the station, Crawford remarks on the noticeable difference between the people's reactions to the police officers and the firefighters. Had the police been the first to spot the steaming auto and pulled in to offer their help, it is likely they'd have received a much more lukewarm reception — perhaps even a chilly one — than the firefighters.

"The thing with us is we always come to help," Crawford says. "If people need help, they know we'll come. The police have got a tough job. They want to help too, but they've got to make tough decisions. If they show up, it means someone there's probably guilty of something and they're not happy to see them. They've got a real tough job."

Night falls and the firefighters enjoy their dinner as darkness settles around the firehouse. A call comes in for Engine 14 and they are soon out the door and heading east on 33rd. They pull up to the address, where someone has called in a report of a seizure. The firefighters are, as usual, first on the scene and walk up the short stretch of concrete leading to a tall, narrow, dark house. A thin woman with large, soft eyes is there to open the door and begins leading the men up a winding — and pitch-black — staircase.

"Lights!" Wells shouts from the back of the procession. "Can we get some lights?"

"There are no lights!" the woman hollers down from above, and the firefighters carefully trudge up the steep, darkened steps, their medical bags bumping against the walls. The rooms in the upstairs residence are dimly lit as the firefighters make their way in. They pass a living room devoid of furniture, save for a small television sitting on an overturned cardboard box. In a bedroom, they find a gangly, young black boy sitting on a mattress that rests on the floor. He is wearing nothing but a pair of black mesh shorts. His large, soft eyes bulge beneath worried eyebrows, and his lower lip droops in fear at the scene in which he suddenly finds himself.

The firefighters find out the boy is eleven, and he continually looks toward his mother for assurance as the firefighters calmly ask him questions about how he's feeling. Crawford jokes around with him in an attempt to get the boy to relax, but to no avail. He mostly just nods or shakes his head once in answer to their questions, his eyes riveted on his mother the entire time. She is leaning on the wall just inside the door, and she tells the firefighters her son threw up and seemed to be seizing up. She said he'd been eating junk food all day and just had a dinner of macaroni and cheese and chicken. He does not seem at all sick now, only frightened. Wright asks the woman if she has gotten after the boy or disciplined him at all tonight, and she says yes, she verbally scolded him shortly before he got sick. The poor kid was apparently so upset about drawing his mother's ire that he vomited.

"I have four kids myself, and sometimes when you get into it with them, they can throw up," Wright explains to the woman as the paramedics appear through the door. "He'll be all right."

Crawford finally gets the boy to crack a smile.

"You going to play football when you grow up?" Crawford asks him.

He nods.

"You going to play for the Vikings?"

The boy thinks for a second, and a proud grin lights his face.

"Tampa Bay," he says.

After filling the paramedics in, the firefighters begin making their way back down the steps toward the rig. One of the paramedics follows them down and asks the firefighters if they wouldn't mind sticking around until they have finished making their own diagnosis of the boy. Several people threw rocks at their ambulance as they made their way to the house, she says, and they are a bit nervous about being in the neighborhood at this point in the night so soon after the riot. The firefighters are not particularly happy about acting as security for the ambulance, but they wait for a few minutes in their rig as the paramedics finish with their duties. Wright mentions that he's amazed people would hurl rocks at an ambulance on its way to help somebody.

Having finished with the boy, the paramedics appear through the door of the house and wave their thanks to the firefighters. As Wells steers the fire engine back into the warm night and aims it toward the station, Wright thinks again about the idea of someone hurling a rock at an emergency vehicle on its way to help someone. It seems utterly senseless to him, and he shakes his head just a little. And then he rolls up his window.

ANSWERING THE BELL

Captain Cherie Penn has steel in her eyes today. With her military training — eight years in the Navy and six more in the Air Force reserves — and the serious professionalism she brings to the job, her demeanor is often stoic and no-nonsense, but she also usually leaves a little room for levity. In down time around the station, though often quiet, she is rarely unapproachable and can be quick with an eye-twinkling smile when the firefighters are kidding around, even if she rarely joins in herself. But on this day, Penn seems fully withdrawn from the social construct within the firehouse. She is physically very present as she moves about the station with her usual gliding, athletic stride, making sure all is as it should be at the beginning of the shift. But there is also a detachedness — a quietly humming barrier that keeps the others in the house from intruding on her most immediate space. While her demeanor is not the primary source of the tension that hangs over the station, it is certainly the most apparent indicator that things are slightly off kilter at Station 14 today.

Ladder 10 and its crew have gone downtown to the maintenance facility to have work done on the aerial, which broke down at a fire the previous evening. The void created by the giant rig and its crew lends an extra hollowness to the station. The warm morning sunshine seems somehow confined to the outside, like a recently disciplined but loyal dog sitting on the other side of the porch door, wondering when, if ever, it will be allowed back inside. Dan Schultz and Troy Bjornstad, a rookie, are sitting in the dining room discussing Bjornstad's recent trip to Vietnam. Penn slips in quietly, sits down, and picks up a section of the newspaper. But after just a few seconds, she is up again and slips out as quietly as she came. Schultz says he hasn't seen Penn smile once during the last four shifts. Bjornstad, less attuned to the recent issues that have Penn rankled, continues with his story about the royal treatment he and his American friends received at the nightclubs in Saigon as Penn shuffles up the steps to her office.

The main reason Penn is on edge has to do with a recent dispute between two firefighters, including one that happened to be under her command. It is a problem that should have and could have been handled by the in-house hierarchy, but instead one of the firefighters took the dispute directly to the higher-ups downtown. It reflected negatively on Penn's ability to keep her troops in line, and, more fundamentally, the chain of command was skirted. Rank was broken. The men and women in the firehouses appreciate their freedom to air grievances as much as anyone else in the workforce, but when the proper channels are evaded, things often get messier than they were in the first place. Soon things get blown out of proportion, and a small personal quarrel between firefighters, if handled improperly, can end up irking the higher echelons downtown and casting an undeserved poor light on front-line officers. It also causes the rank and file to grumble.

So the A shift has begun its day ready to work, but with something less than its usual enthusiasm.

Ladder 10 returns from the shop and goes back into service just after noon. Rather than back the rig into the house, the crew decides to head out for a building familiarization. Crews from all the stations in the city spend some time nearly every day walking through local buildings to get an idea of what kind of hazards and pitfalls they might face, should they ever have to respond to a fire call there. This is a particularly vital procedure in some of the older parts of town, where buildings were built without the benefit of contemporary fire safety and exit laws. With Julie Caouette in the till, Mark Anderson steers the truck north to a small stucco cube of a corner grocery store and adjoining laundromat. An aging, portly man with rough, olive-colored skin and a younger, leaner man who might be his son are working behind the counter and seem a bit disconcerted that four firefighters have just entered and asked to take a look around their premises. But they smile and say go ahead. There is not much to look at upstairs, just several short, narrow aisles filled mostly with junk food. Anderson asks if there is a basement. There is, the older man says and points the way, and the crew heads down a half-dozen old but sturdy steps into a small and poorly lit dungeon of a basement with low ceilings. The firefighters play their flashlights around in the gloom and locate the electrical and gas shutoff points. Electrical wires bundled together and further insulated with cobwebs snake around the unfinished ceiling overhead. There is not much else down here except for some old cardboard boxes and a five-gallon plastic tub of industrial adhesive. The fire danger is not bad, but there would be plenty of fuel for flames to chew on should they ever ignite down here.

Their walk-through complete, the crew heads back upstairs. Someone points out that the bottom five steps are made of old wood planking. If a fire ever gets going good down here, there might not be any steps left to help reach it by the time fire crews arrive. At the top of the steps is a back exit barred shut by a long, thick piece of wood. Anderson clamps on to the door with his big mitts and tests its sturdiness with a hard shake. It doesn't budge.

"That's going to be hard to get through," admits Anderson, whose axe is among the most devastating in the city.

Back outside, a wiry little black man with a small drip of a ponytail and two kids are admiring the equipment on the truck.

"Oh wow," the man exclaims when he sees the Jaws of Life. "That's what you guys use to cut things, right? The Jaws of Life, right?"

"Yeah, that's it," Anderson says as he sits down on a step to wait for Elondo Wright, who lives nearby and has walked over to his house.

"Look at that," the man says to the kids, each of whom is clutching one of his hands. "That's what they use to get people out of cars and stuff."

The man realizes they are blocking the sidewalk for an elderly white man and a little girl.

"Oops, excuse us," the wiry man says.

"No, no, we're just here to look at the fire truck, too," the old man replies.

So the white man and the black man begin moving back and forth along the apparatus, pointing things out to the kids and grinning, equally enamored with the big rig.

Wright returns a few minutes later with his four children in tow. They're wearing nametags from a church activity from which they have recently returned. Wright's wife, Greta, also crosses the street behind them, a bit more slowly now that she's a full eight months pregnant. Someone jokes that they recently saw a TV special that showed newly born baby elephants getting nutrients by eating their mother's dung. Everyone laughs, including Greta, a pretty woman with blonde hair and happy blue eyes. Everyone says their good-byes and Ladder 10 takes back to the streets.

After a stop at Kowalski's, Anderson and Caouette steer the truck to a Chinese restaurant near 42nd Avenue and I-94. The crew spots Engine 14 rolling up the street toward them. The engine drops Penn off, then heads on down the street, apparently headed for the grocery store itself. Penn is no more than a hundred feet from the ladder truck, but she marches into the restaurant without so much as a nod. Without even having heard the comment Schultz made just a couple hours earlier, Anderson notes that he hasn't seen her smile but once in the last four shifts.

Back at the station a short while later, several of the firefighters are in the dining room eating their lunches when someone wonders aloud if the trip the engine took down to City Hall, which houses the department's offices, in the morning had anything to do with Penn's mood.

"I don't know nothing, and I don't want to know," someone else says.

"I'm just sitting here eating my sandwich," another says, not looking up.

That ends the discussion. It is clear that everyone is concerned about Penn and the issues she is dealing with, but they also know that much of it is out of their control now, so they don't want to spend too much time worrying or gossiping about it. They must simply trust that the department's officers will clean up the mess. The firefighters will focus on doing their job.

It's about two-thirty and the ladder has just returned from a run to a house on Colfax, where an old man had locked himself in a room. They were almost on the scene when dispatch came over the radio and said the man had gotten free.

"He must have busted out," Wright says.

"Or his old lady let him out," Anderson jokes.

The rig is back in place and hooked in to the battery chargers. No one else is on the apparatus floor except Penn, who hits a button to open the doors in front of the engine. The sunlight rushes in and bathes the red nose of the rig. Penn slowly wheels a chair to the door and sits down. She sits unmoving for some time, her calm eyes watching the occasional car roll by.

Twenty minutes later she has gone back upstairs, and Jay Wells is sitting in her chair, munching on a large green apple. Three teenage boys from the neighborhood show up and start talking sports — who's going to be good in football, when practice starts, who's going to be the starters.

"We've already had some captain's practices," the biggest of the three explains to Wells, "but the only one there so far was Travis, you know, that kid who got shot, and Carlo, and that other kid with the black jeep. Oh, what's his name?"

The other two boys are younger, brothers in their early teens, and both still have a layer of baby fat. One starts teasing the other about only playing on special teams.

"Man, you're sorry. You're *sorry!*"

The other boy's brow falls, and he looks unsure of how to defend himself. Wells won't let the boy's esteem take this hit, however. He wheels in his chair and shuts the other boy up. "Now, he isn't sorry. He isn't sorry." The boy's chin comes back up and Wells grins. "But someone done lied to me and I ain't too happy about that. I am wondering about this special teams. I thought someone said he was a starter."

The boy smiles again. "I never said I was a starter."

Wells grins broadly and baits him. "You didn't tell me you were a starter?"

"No, I didn't.""Now come on. You didn't tell me you were a starter?"

"I said I started sometime, but I didn't start all the time. I never said I started all the time. But I started sometimes."Wells tilts back in his chair and rolls his neck back, looking at the boy out of the corner of his eyes. Then he laughs. They both laugh.

Less than an hour later, Penn calls the crews from both rigs to the apparatus floor. She gathers everyone around near the tail end of the ladder truck and begins going through various ways to tie knots when attaching them to portable ladders. She speaks calmly, clearly, and with her usual professionalism. The others are paying very close attention, nodding in recognition of the various knots, blurting out answers to her questions, and stepping in one at a time to tie the knots themselves. They know being able to perform these simple tasks can mean the difference between a successful rescue and a catastrophe for endangered civilians and firefighters alike, so they watch the captain with the gravity of a group of medical students watching their first open-heart surgery. They take extra time on the knot used to perform an "auditorium" ladder raise, which is used only in cases where there is no solid wall upon which to prop the ladder.

Next, they move on to ways to lower people trapped in upper floors down the ladders. Ideally, two firefighters would go up and one would enter the floor and tie a rope around the civilian's legs and ankles, then remain in the potentially dangerous area to control the rope while the other firefighter carried the victim down. They also practice various ways to brace the victims depending on their state of consciousness. But firefighters know that there may be instances in which there is not enough time to go through every one of these steps.

"These are guidelines to help you if you get stumped, but it's not etched in stone," Penn says. "If we need to get someone down quickly," she pauses, then utters the rest of the sentence with great confidence, "we are going to get them down, one way or another."

Mrs. Lamb strolls in through the front door wearing a colorful sundress and toting a large jar of homemade pickles for the firefighters. As Mrs. Lamb passes into the kitchen, the lesson continues. Penn picks up a large, long yellow bag about the size of a golf club bag and pulls a strip of thick, white nylon rope out of it. She asks how long the rope in this bag is. Eyebrows knit together as everyone stares at the bag and tries to recall the exact length of the rope inside. Wright pipes up first.

"Seventy feet."

No response from Penn.

"One-twenty," Wright tries again.

Nothing. A pause.

"No, seventy."

"Is it one-fifty?" someone asks.

Wright again: "One-fifty. No, it's one-twenty."

Another pause. Still Wright: "Yep, one-twenty. No, seventy. One-twenty. One-twenty. One-fifty!"

Wright and some of the others start to chuckle softly as they realize that he's stumped and now just hoping to get Penn to react to one of his numbers. Penn does react — with a small smile. As Wright continues his guesses, Penn's smile spreads into a full grin. It's the first smile some of them have seen in a long time, and it is a welcome sight.

It's just after five-thirty, and the training time has long since ended. Bjornstad is in the clutch tonight and calls over the station intercom that dinner is ready. Schultz, Anderson, Julie Caouette, and Shawn Modahl join Bjornstad and scoop big piles of spiced ground beef from a massive black skillet onto white tortilla shells in the kitchen. They then pile plenty of other toppings on top of their tacos and move into the dining room to begin eating. Conversation is light as the firefighters begin mowing through their food, but there would not have been much time to delve into any particular topic anyway, as the alarm sounds. Even tones. It's a fire, and everyone's going.

The five eating dinner file quickly through the door to the apparatus floor, where Wells is already firing up the engine. Boots are pulled on as the dispatcher's voice relays the vitals. 3105 Girard. A car fire. The engine blares into the street and heads east, the truck right behind it. As the rigs turn on to Lowry, the heavy smell of smoke flows in through the open windows of the cabs. The sirens wail through the intersections, and the rigs swing on to Girard. Immediately, an old white Dodge van can be seen as the source of the billowing, acrid clouds. The engine pulls past the van and the ladder stops just short. Black smoke is rolling from the hood, and fluid dripping from the van's engine is on fire. There is no one in the van.

Caouette and Modahl jump from the truck and, axes in hand, move to the front of the van and begin swinging away at the front of the hood just above the grill while the engine crew prepares the line. Bjornstad has the nozzle and waits several yards from the van as Caouette and Modahl work. The axe heads slamming into metal resound with loud bangs in the quiet neighborhood. The hood pops open and Bjornstad opens up with the hose. The fire hisses and sputters but is no match for the sudden gush of water. The fire has reached inside the van, so Anderson busts the driver's side window in order to get the door unlocked and opened. He then reaches in with the Halligan tool and pries away the cover near the dash that opens to the engine. Water from the hose now has more room to roam and gushes into the front seats of the van. The driver's door hangs open, exposing a pile of soft, blue glass sitting on a sodden, white, furry seat cover.

Wright is chopping at the swinging doors on the back of the van, and they soon come partially open. The others bring their axes to bear on the hinges, and soon the back of the van has been torn open. The fire has not spread this far, but the firefighters check to make sure there are no gas cans or other flammables inside.

Kids have come running from both ends of the block to see what all the commotion is about. They watch with bulging eyes as the firefighters work. An old man who lives in the house directly across from the van trundles down his walkway and sits on a step and begins snapping pictures with a small point-and-shoot camera. On the other side of the street, a woman standing on her porch begins yelling to the firefighters, but she is not easily heard over the water that is still being poured into the van and the idling fire engines.

She finally catches Penn's attention, and the captain moves onto the steps and asks the woman if this is her van. She says no, and she has a look of shocked disbelief on her face as she explains to Penn what she witnessed. She saw a man getting into the van, and she noticed it was on fire. She says she began calling out to the man, who then calmly got out, grabbed some things from the back of the van, walked to another car and drove away, leaving the van to its fiery fate. Penn nods and informs the woman that an arson investigator will want to talk to her and will arrive soon.

Bjornstad is still attacking the van's motor with the hose. Thick cascades of molten steel have dribbled down the front of the van and pooled on the ground, looking like wax from a candle that has spilled over its top. The engine won't stop smoking, so Bjornstad removes the oil cap and air filter and fills the motor with water. This seems to finally have the fire on its knees, so Engine 14 takes up its hose and follows Ladder 10 back to the station. Anderson inhaled a snootful of smoke while doing his work in the front seat of the van, and he is coughing and hocking up mucus and spitting it out the window.

"Gotta get that shit out of there," he says.

Wright is also hacking a bit and suggests that next time they put on their oxygen masks before delving into a vehicle showing so much heavy smoke.

"Because that didn't taste too good," he says.

"It never does," Anderson says, then hacks and spits again.

Grease from the spiced meat has coagulated on the plates containing the dormant and cooled tacos, but the fire seems to have loosened everyone's collars a bit after an otherwise tense day. The humor begins to flow more liberally and everyone is a bit more relaxed now that their hair and navy blue undershirts have a little sweat on them. Hard rock music is blaring from the TV as a pro wrestling match is getting set to start, and Caouette asks Schultz if he will dance for everybody. While working as a bartender at a restaurant prior to becoming a firefighter, Schultz and the rest of the floor staff would occasionally have to jump onto the restaurant's tables and perform dance moves from the '50s, one of which Caouette is mocking right now. Schultz is in the other room preparing to grab some more dinner, and Anderson turns and shouts, "Come on, shake your butt for us!" Everyone's laughter is hearty and comes deep from the lungs. Schultz enters and only smiles as he sits at the table.

The firefighters polish off their tacos and some go for seconds. Movie stars Jennifer Aniston and Brad Pitt are being featured on an entertainment TV program, and some of the guys mock Pitt's new beard and effeminate, pretty-boy looks. The phone rings. It's for Modahl — someone reminding him that former University of Minnesota wrestling heavyweight Brock Lesnar is going to be on the tube in a pro wrestling match with Hulk Hogan tonight. Some of the guys begin making plans to tune in. Lesnar is one of the most astoundingly muscled men on the planet, a walking stack of human protein. Lesnar is the firefighters' kind of guy. Brad Pitt, as it turns out, is not.

It's shortly after dinner and the kitchen and dining room have been scrubbed and mopped. Caouette begins sharpening an axe blade. Schultz is outside mowing the station's large green lawn when the engine is called out for a medical run. A young boy has been hit by a car while riding his bike. The emergency vehicles screech onto the scene, but the boy only has some bumps and bruises to show for it, and the engine returns quickly to quarters. More time leaks away, and the firefighters are just beginning to congregate around the station's TVs to watch Lesnar's wrestling match. Most everyone seems interested — everyone except Anderson, who is downstairs in the weight room watching "The Munsters."

The match is about to begin when a fire call comes in. It's another vehicle fire, and this time the fire engines have quite a bit further to travel than they did for the last one. The engine rolls first, with the ladder a short distance back. The car, a Pontiac two-door, is parked in front of 2709 Third Street, and the rigs again move east on Lowry. The sun has fully set, and the rigs' red lights wash across the old houses and small business structures as they pass. It is a beautiful night and there are a lot of people hanging out on street corners and stoops on Lowry. As the ladder makes the turn south onto Lyndale, a skinny, middle-aged man with droopy eyes and sunglasses clinging low to the tip of his nose steps into the street and begins to cross, seemingly oblivious to the truck's pulsing sirens. A long, brown cigarette dangles from his lips and, as he takes his first few stumbling steps, it is clear that alcohol or some other substance has woven a shroud around his mind. Anderson blows the man's mental fog away with a blast of the air horn. The man looks up, then stumbles backwards to the corner, just in time for the truck to make the turn without hitting him. Amazingly, the man's expression has not changed from its inebriated deadpan, even though he has just about committed his own unwitting suicide. He just stands, wobbling, on the corner. Once the truck has past, he staggers back into the street.

The truck howls down Lyndale, and the crew hears Penn's call to dispatch that they've got a vehicle fully involved. As the ladder joins the scene, the engine crew has already begun connecting the foam attachment to its line, and Bjornstad is soon on all fours spraying the slurping white liquid underneath the vehicle as flame licks out from the sides of the hood. The rookie is aggressive and strong. Some of the more veteran firefighters have also noted that he seems to have a good head on his shoulders. One even mentions that the rookie could be good captain material one day.

"Something's going to get broke," says Wright as he hops from the captain's seat of the truck and grabs an axe. The ladder crew begins chopping away at the front of the hood, which is putting up stern resistance. Anderson steps forward and blasts the hood with a half-dozen quick, powerful chops. On the last three hacks, he connects with the car's horn mechanism, and it responds with a series of blaps and bleats, like a wild animal begging for mercy. The Pontiac's pain will soon be over, though, as the hood is now up and has exposed a roaring fire. Bjornstad makes short work of it with the foam. Caouette clamps on to the battery cables with a long-handled bolt cutter and begins snipping away. The battery protests and spits several long streams of glowing orange sparks at her, but finally it is disconnected. Bjornstad continues soaking the engine with foam.

The usual collection of curious families and teens has gathered to watch the show, and a handful of boys have snuck up close to the vehicle, where the firefighters can't see them. A few women who must be their mothers spot them, however, and they scream frantically at the boys to get away from the car. The boys at first don't respond and the women continue to shriek. Slowly, reluctantly, the youths pull back to a safe distance. Two of the teens that were watching have lost interest and begin walking back down Third as the ladder begins its slow trip back to quarters. As the truck turns the corner where the two teenagers are walking, one of them looks up and shouts, "You guys are heroes! You save the world!"

He has a serious look on his face and seems to mean what he says. His friend then pipes up. "Yeah, you guys are heroes!" but in the next breath decides to get cute. "Yeah, you're not *my* heroes, but you're *somebody's* heroes." It is the playful and mildly foolish irreverence that adolescents begin to show as they enter their rebellious stage, and this kid has probably just said it to make his buddy laugh. It works, and both guffaw as they stride off down the street. The firefighters just smile.

Back on Lowry, there are a lot of people loitering on the streets. Most are moving about in small packs of three or four, while others are just sitting and watching traffic pass. Anderson notes that there seem to be more people out than usual tonight, and that could mean a long night for the fire department. As the truck motors past the public library on Lowry, the firefighters watch as two police offers make an arrest. One is handcuffing a young man while the other is sweeping the concrete steps that lead up to the library with his flashlight as if he's looking for something — evidence, maybe, that the youth might have thrown.

"Uh-oh," Anderson quips. "He must have been looking at porn on the library Internet."

Back at the station, the vigorous work of the two car fires seems to have been good medicine for the mood of the house. Several of the firefighters spend the rest of the evening watching TV in the dining room and chatting casually. Modahl and Schultz also form an interesting spectacle that most people wouldn't expect to see in a firehouse. The stocky men are bent over the kitchen table, pulling pins from a small red pin cushion and inserting them carefully at measured intervals into a large piece of heavy fabric, which happens to be printed with teddy bears wearing yellow jackets and blue baseball caps ("It was either this or ducks," Schultz explains blithely). Caouette is setting up a sewing machine she has brought to the station with her, and the three of them are sewing the fabric into curtains for the kids' bathroom in Schultz's home. Soon Caouette is sewing away as Schultz stands behind her, hands on hips, watching closely. Some of the other firefighters give Schultz a mild ribbing as they see the project that's under way. Some guys might not want their buddies and coworkers to see such a spectacle, but such considerations usually go out the window around here when it means one firefighter lending the other a helping hand. And most of the guys on the department are secure enough with their masculinity that they can poke pins through slabs of fabric with cuddly little bears all over it without losing face — just so long as it doesn't become a habit.

Caouette finishes up the sewing as the others watch the recent remake of the movie "Shaft" on TV. One by one, everyone strolls off to bed as the night deepens. Caouette is one of the last to remain awake, and with her last reserves of energy draining away as she leans on the ladder truck, her voice thick with exhaustion in the quiet hush of the night, she talks about the day gone by. Just like any workplace, she says, sometimes people don't get along all the time and it ends up affecting everybody. But despite it all, they stick together to complete the important tasks at hand. Ultimately, what matters to them all is doing the job.

"There were some bad vibes here for a while today, but everything will be okay," she explains. "Everyone will come back for the next shift ready to go. Some days are just better than others, I guess."

ANSWERING THE BELL

"They're about to crack a deuce," Elondo Wright predicts as he marches into the dining room, where some of the other firefighters are watching "Monday Night Football." He cocks his head slightly to one side as he says it, to show just how confident he is in his prediction. "Better get ready on the truck, 'cause they're gonna crack a deuce any minute now."

A deuce. As in two-alarm fire. Also known as a 2-2 in fire-service speak. Multiple alarm fires are rare, and there were only twenty-three deuces in the city a year ago. But if Wright thought his forecast might elicit a dissenting response from his comrades, none is forthcoming. A house is burning about six miles away in northeast Minneapolis, and they have been listening to the same radio transmissions he has as they've come in over the station intercom. The factors that might cause the chief in charge to strike a second alarm are indeed beginning to stack up. The house is two stories, and old. There is a lot of smoke coming from multiple floors, and the house is so cluttered with junk that the first-alarm crews on scene are having trouble even getting through the doors, and those that do gain entry are not getting far. And they are catching glimpses of blooming flame through the dense, dark smoke in multiple locations. These facts are being broadcast for every sta-

145

tion in the city to hear by the captains and chief running the show. The crews at Station 14 have had a fairly slow day, relatively speaking, but when they have been called out, there has been fire to fight. They responded along with Engine 16 to a car fire midway through the morning. After that, things rolled along quietly for several hours until, in reaffirmation of one of the immutable laws of firehouse life, the bells rang out again just as the firefighters had settled into their evening meal. Tom Rogalski wore the apron tonight, and all six diners were forking their way through bowls of salad greens and overflowing plates of seasoned chicken halves, steamed broccoli, and baked potatoes the size of small footballs when they were sent scurrying for the apparatus floor. That run turned out to be a heavily smoking dryer fire, and first-arriving Engine 20 handled it with a ventilation assist from Ladder 10. After Engine 14 returned to quarters, Captain Kris Lemon hauled the ladder company's food plates into the kitchen and stored them in one of the large, warm ovens to help keep Rogalski's hard work in the kitchen from degenerating into plates of cold leftovers. Some twenty minutes later, the truckies returned and made short work of the birds. Gullets well-stuffed, the firefighters sank into chairs in front of the TVs to watch the Green Bay Packers take on the Miami Dolphins. The initial 911 call for the fire they are now listening to came from a neighbor who saw smoke curling out of the basement windows of the house on Lincoln Street Northeast. Dispatch sent out the alarm to Stations 2 and 11.

Engine 11 is screaming north on Central, driver Craig Lasley weaving the rig from one lane to the next through traffic as acting captain Al Daher steps hard on the wailing siren to give motorists one more ear-splitting incentive to get out of the way. In the backseat, rookie Tom Hupp is pulling on his hood and helmet and securing his turnout coat. Daher does the same as Engine 11 careens around the corner and on to Broadway. Right on their tail is Rescue 9, the massive heavy rescue truck that shares quarters with Engine 11. Dana Declouet is riding in charge of the rescue company, with David Vincent, Jackson Millikan, and Robert Sayers under his command.

Both rigs lean as they wheel around the corner onto Lincoln, the heavy smoke from the fire now evident, silting the air from more than a block away. As the rigs growl to a stop in front of the house, Daher sees fire shooting from the back of the house and radios that fact to dispatch. Lasley climbs down from the driver's seat and immediately goes to work throwing Engine 11 into pump. The Rescue 9 crew will work as the first-in truck company, performing ventilation and helping make entry with axes and hooks.

"Tom, get the line ready!" Daher barks to Hupp, then moves swiftly to the front of the house, climbs three rickety steps, and bangs on the porch door to see if there is any response. Nothing. Daher decides he wants to try and take a first stab at the fire by driving straight in through this door, so he pulls the screen door from its hinges and moves into the enclosed porch. On both sides, Daher is faced with mounds of wood, bicycles, furniture, and cans that have been stuffed into the porch, and he now suspects he's got a junk house on his hands, and that this could end up being a tougher job than it first appeared. His instincts prove correct when Daher attempts to kick open the interior door and it doesn't budge. Hupp is now right behind him with the tank line, and Daher kicks at the door again. It opens, but only slightly. A gust of heated air and smoke rushes out to meet him. But there is too much clutter behind the door to get it open far enough for a person to slip through, so Daher quickly decides to try another entrance and radios to Battalion Chief Jean Kidd that he's got a heavy fire load. The chief calls for a full first-alarm assignment.

Daher and Hupp back out of the porch and head around to the north side of the house, where smoke is billowing from a window. Rescue 9 heads to the back of the house, which faces east, to search for another entry point. Daher and Hupp are able to force the side door open far enough to allow another gale of heat and smoke to blow over them. Declouet and Millikan come back to the side door and go to work forcing it open far enough to squeeze part of the way through. Just inside the door, they see stacks of paint and oil cans and other flammables that, luckily, the fire hasn't reached yet. The firefighters quickly pull it all outside to keep it from going up. The rest of the kitchen is piled nearly to the ceiling with milk cartons, golf clubs, shoes, bicycles — dozens and dozens of bicycles — and bicycle parts. It's the junk of a packrat. Pots and pans are everywhere, and there are stacks of wood that reach to the ceiling.

Daher and Hupp can see the orange glow of fire climbing from the floor to the wall eight feet in front of them in the back area of the kitchen, and they open up with their hose and spray the flames and the walls. The water is met by a wall of heat that causes it to expand into roiling clouds of steam. Both wipe their gloved hands across their masks to clear their vision. It soon begins to cool just a bit, but Hupp and Daher are fighting from a pinched position between the door and the wall. So they pull back to allow Rescue 9 to go to work on the door, and it takes some time to get it out of the way. There is no room to swing an axe, so they have to pry at the hinges with their tools until they give way. Once the door is off, Declouet sends Vincent and Sayers downstairs to see if they can find anymore fire. They soon return saying there is a lot of heat down there, but they can't see any fire for the smoke. Daher and Hupp move back in with the line as Declouet and Millikan go back to smashing out any windows they can reach to let the smoke out. With all the heat and combustible material all around the fire, as well as the influx of oxygen from the windows, the flames kick back up.

"Don't get far from me, Hupper!" Daher yells through his oxygen mask. "There's too much clutter in here, and if we get too far in, it's going to be hard to get out!"

By this time, Engine 2 has arrived and pulled down the block to relay water from the hydrant through a supply line. Dan Schultz is driving for Engine 2 today, and he gets the relay pump going while his captain, Tim Baynard, leads firefighter Tim Evavold toward Engine 11. They hook in with a backup line and begin stretching it toward the house. A man approaches them and meets them in the yard.

"My uncle lives there," he says to Baynard.

"Do you know if he's in there right now?" Baynard asks.

"I think he's in there," the man says anxiously. "He may be back towards the kitchen area. That's normally where he's at.

That's where he sleeps."

Baynard relays the information to Kidd, who is directing operations. She radios to all crews that there may be a victim inside as Baynard and Evavold move quickly to the side door. The worried man tries to follow them, and Baynard finally has to turn and hold him back.

"Stay back," Baynard says. "Let us do our job. We'll find him."

When Daher hears the radio call that there may be a victim inside, his adrenaline goes through the roof, but he is only able to slowly nudge his way around the junk piles just inside the door, and he can't see much. Whoever lives here has filled their home with so much junk that there is no way to navigate through it except through very narrow aisles. And the smoke is so heavy that flashlights don't help at all. They illuminate the path ahead about as well as a car's high beams in a dense fog.

"I can't see a damn thing," Daher mutters to himself.

The chief has patiently allowed her crews to ply their way into and around the scene as they sought the seat of the fire. The likelihood that the fire would soon require a second alarm — two more engines and two more ladders — was as evident to Kidd as it is to the firefighters listening in at Station 14. But rather than call in four new companies too early, she allowed the first-responding crews the necessary time to battle their way to the areas in the smoke-filled house where the flames lurk. Pulling the trigger too early on additional alarms can send new crews crashing into the backs of others already on scene, creating a tangled muddle of personnel and equipment. But once the first assignment companies have staked out attack positions, the chief radios dispatch to up the response to a second alarm. This will bring in enough manpower to help keep the department well ahead of the fire. At Station 14, the crew of Ladder 10 heard Kidd call for the deuce and is already suiting up when the bell goes off.

Declouet and Millikan decide to try and clear a path of entry through the back door to search for the victim. The interior of the back of the house is as badly cluttered and claustrophobic as every other point where the crews have tried to get inside. They begin dragging mattresses, wood, crates, bikes, and chunks of old furniture out through the back and tossing it all into the yard. But the going is slow, and they are only able to cut their way in at a rate of about one foot per minute.

"What is all this shit?" Millikan barks, verbally venting his frustration. "This is ridiculous. There's just too much in here."

Millikan hopes someone is out there clearing away all the debris they're ejecting, otherwise it could be piled up so high as to make it hard for them to get out. With all the time that's ticking away during this battle to gain entry, he also wonders if the fire is getting ahead of them. The general rule firefighters live by is that a fire doubles in size with each passing minute. If things go from bad to worse, everyone might soon be ordered out for a surround-and-drown fight, but the crews on scene are determined to make a good stop on this fire. Soon the high-pitched whistles that indicate both Millikan and Declouet have blown through most of the oxygen in their tanks add to the chaos. So they head outside, guzzle a quick sports drink, strap on new air bottles, then begin chipping away through the back doorway again. Daher and Hupp are replacing their bottles, too, as the second-in companies keep up the fight. After about ten minutes of going toe-to-toe with the fire in the kitchen, Daher and Hupp directed their nozzle at flames through the basement windows for several minutes before their air finally gave out.

Declouet and Millikan take another crack at trying to find the man inside. Ladder 7 is plying its way through the front of the house with the same goal in mind. As they pick their way through the resident's collected debris, Millikan thinks about how, in most houses this size, they could search a floor from front to back in about thirty seconds. Here, they are on their second air bottle and they've barely made it ten feet. They finally make it close enough to another door into the kitchen and Millikan wrenches it open. There is just enough room for Millikan, who is more slightly built than Declouet, to wriggle through. The intense heat that washes over him causes him instinctively to drop to all fours. When he looks up, he sees one of the most amazing sights he's ever seen in

150

his life.

A refrigerator is standing in the middle of the floor in the jumbled kitchen. From around the sides of the refrigerator, tentacles of long, wispy, green, blue, and orange flame are reaching out toward him. They lick hypnotically at the air in front of his facemask. Millikan was a flight attendant before becoming a firefighter, and these mesmerizing flames remind him of one international flight he worked. The captain called him to the cockpit to view an amazing visual orchestra of the Northern Lights that was flowing above the plane. It was breath-taking, and it looked a lot like this.

Millikan snaps out of his brief trance, and both he and Declouet are beginning to realize that, with all the heat and smoke in this house, if anyone is inside, they are likely dead by now. Rescue 1 is also on scene now and searching other areas of the house, so far in vain. Millikan and Declouet realize it's time for them to think about their own safety. They have done their best to find the victim, but they are inside a smoky, burning, cramped environment without a line to protect them if something goes wrong. Millikan turns and shouts through his mask that there are flames and intense heat in the kitchen.

"Okay, let's back it out," Declouet orders.

Millikan tries to turn and squeeze back through the door, but each way he twists, another piece of his gear gets caught on something. His heart rate races and his chest seizes up slightly. But he quickly catches the panic by its throat, remembers his training and tells himself to stay calm. You got in here, you can get out, he tells himself. He slowly and carefully gets himself to the opening and wriggles back through. As he and Declouet make their way to the door to the outside, a pile of junk shifts and forces it shut before they can reach it. Utterly exhausted and frustrated, they dig their way through the debris and finally exit the crammed house and step into the cool, fall night air. Their most recent foray has drained their oxygen again and they trudge down the street for fresh tanks and to guzzle another sports drink. Through all the communications zipping back and forth between the captains and the chief, a transmission from inside the house comes through loud and clear for everyone to hear: "We've got a victim on the first floor."

Captain Tom Rogalski and the Ladder 10 crew hear the confirmation of a victim ripple across the department airwaves as they pull into the staging area at the intersection of Lincoln and 14th. Engine 1, Engine 19, and Ladder 4 are all arriving at about the same time. Assistant Fire Chief Ulysses Seal and Deputy Chief James Rodger have also arrived to help oversee operations. The police have blocked off traffic access to Lincoln from several different directions. A whole block, and then some, is now filled with fire rigs — eleven in all, plus a salvage truck, a mobile command unit, and the chiefs' vehicles. The entire area is pulsating with the crimson-tinged electricity of their warning lights. Rescue 9 has elevated a massive bank of flood lights into the air just in front of the house, and when they snap on, the nighttime darkness flees to reveal an urgently working scene of firefighters as they continue to pull junk from the house and battle the flames within. The streets and yard are a highway map of hose. Smoke continues to pour from the house and mingles with diesel fumes from the idling fire engines in the nostrils of onlookers.

Rogalski leads Mark Anderson, Shawn Modahl, and Siobhan Mullen down the street toward the house with axes and hooks in hand. After making a quick scan of the house from the front and sides, Rogalski sends his crew to retrieve a length of ground ladder and a smaller roof ladder.

"Let's get a hole in the roof for these guys," Rogalski commands, and soon they are making their way to the top of the house, where they go to work chopping holes to let the smoke and heat out.

Crews inside have dug their way into the basement and found more of the same junk stacked to eye level. The basement ceiling has partially collapsed and the refrigerator in the upstairs kitchen has fallen through, but it only dropped about two feet, as it is now being held up by the junk piles.

The flames are soon out, and the firefighters find that they were burning heavily around a large, old-fashioned, wood-burning stove in the basement. Neighbors who are watching from outside say the reclusive elderly gentleman who lives here would often be seen carting wood back to his home on the back of his bike. He probably stockpiled whatever wood he could find to heat his house through the long Minnesota winter. The area around the stove will undoubtedly be one of the first spots the fire investigators examine.

Declouet and Millikan head back into the house from the side to help the crews who are sweeping throughout in search of areas where the fire might be hiding. The going is slow through the narrow aisles of junk, but the firefighters do their best to check every crevice, and to climb up over mounds of wood to get a good look behind them. Through the haze, Declouet spots a stairwell leading up to the second floor. He feels his way over, and just before reaching the first step, someone calls out to him.

"Watch out for that body!"

Declouet stops in his tracks and his gaze drops to the floor. Near his feet is the body of a man lying on his back perpendicular to the steps going upstairs. Through the still-thick haze, Declouet can see the man is just ten feet from the front door, but something, probably the smoke, got him before he could make it out. Declouet's shoulders slump. A nine-year veteran of the department, he has seen a lot. His fellow firefighters know him as a warm-hearted, soft-spoken, and personable man, and the sight of the man's lifeless body sticks Declouet in the heart.

"Poor guy," Declouet mutters to himself.

But there is still work to be done, and Declouet gently steps past the man and begins up the stairs. He and the other firefighters find a few pockets of trapped heat and smoke on the second floor and in the cockloft, but no fire. Ladder 10 soon has two new holes peeled back, and the smoke and heat are flooding upwards.

A few minutes later, Rogalski and his crew are making their way back down the ladder when six firefighters appear through the front door of the house. They are moving quickly and carry a massive, blue plastic tarp with the body of the victim wrapped inside. They carry him to the south of the house and lay him in the middle of a small patch of scraggly trees, offering him some shelter from Rescue 9's floodlights and the prying eyes of neighbors, TV crews, and newspaper photographers.

153

Inside, the first-arriving crews are laying down blankets of foam on all floors of the house. There is so much wood and other fuel still stacked to the ceiling, as well as literally thousands of tiny places for a fire to smolder and hide, that the threat of a rekindle is high. Any firefighters who have been inside know they do not want to have to come back here to do this all over again in a few hours, so they climb on top of and behind piles of junk to get the foam into every nook and cranny.

There is little work left for Ladder 10 to do, so they are released from the scene. Rogalski and Anderson trail behind Modahl and Mullen, who are carrying the ladders. They stop for a few moments near the salvage truck and banter with some of the first-in crewmembers who are refreshing their air tanks at the salvage truck. Several of the firefighters have removed their turnout coats to cool down in the forty-degree air. Their faces and their sweat-soaked, navy blue work T-shirts are barely visible through the heavy plumes of steam swelling from their heated upper bodies.

Ladder 10 arrives back at Station 14 just after ten-thirty, and Anderson brings the rig to a halt out front. Ladder 3's rig occupies Ladder 10's stall in the station, having moved over from Station 7 on Franklin to help keep the North Side covered while Ladder 10 worked the fire. The crews greet each other briefly before Ladder 3 saddles up and heads for home.

The big doors in front of the ladder's bay have been open long enough for the chill November air to infiltrate the station, and the black, wall-mounted radiators throughout the ground floor gurgle and rattle as they try to recover. As usually happens when the temperatures drop in Minnesota, a handful of mice have sought shelter in the station, and one or two are occasionally seen scurrying across the apparatus floor. On the greaseboard in the kitchen, where the firefighters list items that need to be purchased for the station, someone has made the following request:

A cat to catch mice!
A dog to kill cat
Elephant to squash dog
Mouse to get rid of elephant

After the truck is back in place, the firefighters spread back out into the station. Several watch the final minutes of the football game tick away, while others watch news broadcast previews of the impending elections. Tomorrow is mid-term election day across the country, and several races in Minnesota are being hotly contested. The state is also dealing with the recent tragic deaths of Senator Paul Wellstone and seven others in a plane crash in a forested area of northern Minnesota. Former Vice President Walter Mondale has picked up Wellstone's torch and is running a last-minute campaign against Republican Norm Coleman. The race, which could affect which political party has control of the U.S. Senate, has galvanized the state. The election is on the minds and lips of everyone in the state, and political discussions have been prevalent in the firehouse the past several weeks.

The Republicans paraded their big guns — President George W. Bush, First Lady Laura Bush, Vice President Dick Cheney, former New York mayor Rudy Giuliani — through the state the past several days to stump for Coleman, and the Democrats were doing their best to deflect that support from the GOP candidate today. A news station is showing a clip of film actress Jessica Lange speaking at a local rally for Democrats, and she's imploring Minnesotans not to allow "outside interests" to sway their votes.

"What, you mean like Hollywood?" Modahl comments. The firefighters chuckle and nod at his observation as the crowd on TV cheers.

Shortly after eleven, most of the truckies are in bed, and the engine crew follows shortly thereafter. By midnight the firehouse is quiet, save for the occasional snore that grumbles through the dorm. The stillness breaks a few minutes before two in the morning. Click. The lights come on. BEEP beep BEEP beep BEEP beep. A medical run for Engine 14 — the beginning of a busy night. This run is an easy one — a woman with strep throat who's having a little trouble breathing. Kris Lemon, Wright, and Jay Wells meet her on her front porch and wait until the ambulance arrives after they determine she's not in any urgent danger.

Back to the station and back to bed. Twenty minutes after they lie back down, the lights come back on and the tones pulse throughout the dorm.

"Engine 14, with police. One down, 39th and Thomas," the dispatcher calls out. "Time is two forty-one."

One down. Someone is down on the street at the intersection named by the dispatcher, who apparently received some information from a 911 caller who made her wary enough to send the police along with the fire department. Engine 14 does not know what that information was, however, and will have to wait until they get there to see what's going down.

As the truckies roll over in their bunks, the engine crewmembers pull their shoes on, slide the pole, and are out the door again moments later, sirens shrieking in the night. Up Penn and west at the Dowling intersection. One more block and Wells swings the engine up Thomas and to a halt. The corner is dark and quiet. No sign of any disturbance or anyone on the ground as Wells plays the driver's side spotlight around the area. Lemon and Wright search the area on foot with flashlights. Lemon radios dispatch that they are finding nothing.

A pause, then dispatch responds that the call came in from a cell phone, and the victim could be at the corner of Thomas and 40th. Wells hears the message and calls out to Wright, who is still searching down the block to the east. Wright sprints back to the rig and Wells guides it up the street to the corner of 40th.

Still nothing. The firefighters begin another search with their lights. Suddenly three people emerge from dark alley near where Lemon is scouting about. They calmly point her back to the west and say they saw someone lying near the building on the corner. Still sitting in the cab, Wells sees them point and swings the spotlight in that direction. His beam lands on the large, flat outer wall of Maranatha Christian Academy. He directs it to ground level, and the powerful light centers around a man lying on the ground, his head propped against the wall.

"Down there! Down there!" Wells shouts, then slides down from his seat to the street. The ambulance and police have just arrived, and all quickly walk the forty yards from the street corner to the motionless man.

The ground near the wall is coated with a thick mantle of yellow leaves. The man has apparently been thrashing his legs around, as he has cleared out a large semicircle in the leaves around his body. Right now he is completely still, his eyes closed.

Lemon and Wright crouch and begin talking to the man, trying to bring him to consciousness. He finally opens his eyes, bleary and half-glazed, and his body begins to writhe slowly. He tries to speak, but only a few unintelligible grunts tumble from his mouth.

"Are you okay?" Lemon asks. "Are you hurt? Are you hurt anywhere? Do you know how you got here?"

It takes all the man's concentration just to keep his eyes open, and he looks slowly from Lemon to the others around him, the light from their flashlights clearly a shock to his recently slumbering brain. It also becomes clear rather quickly that something else is impairing his thoughts to the point that he can't comprehend what is going on. Confused looks play across his facial features.

It becomes apparent they're not going to get any answers out of him, but they know they can't just leave him here, so Lemon and Wright pull the man to his feet. The two police officers stand nearby, watching intently, ready to intervene if need be. The man is massive, probably about 6-foot-6, his height dwarfing Lemon, his bulk making the stocky Wright look small by comparison. Under his brown jacket, the imposing man is wearing a bright red sweatshirt with a cuddly Christmas teddy bear printed on the front.

One of the paramedics steps forward and helps the firefighters keep the man on his feet as he teeters back and forth. Lemon continues trying to get any information she can from him, but his head simply swivels and bobs as he tries vainly to regain his bearings. Finally, after Lemon asks one more time for his name, he mutters, "Doug."

"Do you know how you got out here, Doug?" Lemon asks.

He stares at her, his lower lip dripping a long thread of saliva.

"Just looking for a place to sleep?" she continues.

He nods once, his eyes closing up again.

"Did you have something to drink tonight, Doug?"

His eyelids lift a few centimeters. He nods.

One of the police officers steps forward and asks if Doug has any identification. No response, so the officer digs into the wobbly man's pockets. All he finds is a few scraps of paper and a porn magazine.

Confident now that Doug is not physically injured, but rather suffering from a long, hard bout with a bottle, the firefighters and paramedics release him to the police. The cops whisk him away in the back of their squad car. The firefighters amble back to their rig and roll back to the station.

"It's that time of year," Lemon says. "We'll have to start picking everybody up. You're not allowed to sleep outside in this cold."

Back at the station, the crew has been back in bed for half an hour when another run comes across the speakers for an epileptic seizure. It's almost four in the morning now. Engine 14 rolls into the street and shortly thereafter pulls up to the house, where a woman on the front porch waves them in.

The first floor of the home is tidy and neatly furnished. The walls are covered with paintings, many of which depict a black Jesus. A mantle above the fireplace is home to small figurines of black angels and a black Santa Claus. The woman of the house is heavyset with a beautiful face and luminous eyes. As she leads the firefighters to the second floor, a young teenage girl watches them from the top of the steps, a look of deep concern stretched across her face.

In the upstairs bedroom, the firefighters find a burly man who appears to be in his late thirties writhing in a fitful sleep on a bed. He is wearing only his boxer shorts, and his sweat has soaked the sheets where he lies. The woman says his name is Charles, and that he does indeed have epilepsy, but he ran out of the medication he takes for it earlier in the day. They are planning on refilling his prescription in the morning, but for now the man looks to be in rough shape as he continues to moan and twist on the bed. The paramedics arrive and appear at the top of the steps.

Suddenly the man's eyes pop open. He seems clear-eyed but confused as to where he is and who all these people are, what they're doing in his bedroom. Lemon and one of the paramedics help him sit up on the bed, and he is unresponsive to the questions they ask of him.

"How are you feeling?" Lemon asks, but gets no response.

After they take his blood pressure, Charles tries to stand up quickly, as if he wants to escape. Lemon and one of the paramedics restrain him and try to settle him down.

"Charles!" his wife shouts. "Charles! Relax, honey! Charles!" But he persists in his attempts to stand.

"Is he usually like this when he comes out of a seizure?" Lemon asks as she holds on tightly to one of his arms.

"Yes," the woman replies.

"Just relax, Charles," Lemon says calmly. "Why don't you lie down?"

"These people want to help you, Charles," his wife says.

But after a few more seconds of struggle, Charles puts more of his muscle into it and is soon on his feet, breaking out of Lemon's grasp. He lunges for the steps, and his wife's pleas are becoming more and more shrill. Wright grabs one of the man's arms and holds him back. Charles looks around the room, his gaze studying the faces of the people around him, but still he does not speak. He sways slightly on his feet, with Wright and Lemon each holding fast to one of his arms.

Charles ignores, or just doesn't understand, the pleas to relax that are raining down upon his ears, and with one great effort tears his arms away from the firefighters one more time. But now he turns away from the stairway and runs around the end of the bed toward a large recliner that is sitting near the window. As his wife continues to shout his name, he stops, looks at her for a moment, then grabs the back of the chair and turns it over.

"He ain't never been like this before," the woman says.

Charles makes another mad stumbling dash for the steps, but Wright, Lemon, and the paramedics are just able to get control of him before he goes crashing through the railing. It takes all their strength to hold him back. Charles has planted his feet and is leaning hard toward the steps.

He relents for a moment and finally speaks his first words since the firefighters arrived: "Gotta...pee."

Everyone in the room relaxes just a bit, and the firefighters smile, but maintain their strong grip.

"Okay, but let us help you down the stairs, Charles," Lemon

says, and soon he is in the first-floor restroom relieving himself for nearly a full minute. Everyone gathers in the living room until he is finished, and his wife meets him at the door, whispering soothing words to calm him down. He staggers out into the living room and the firefighters help him onto the couch. His wife sits next to him and pulls him towards her tightly in her arms, continuing to calm him with her voice. The man now seems fully lucid, if tired, and the paramedics tell the firefighters they can handle it from here. Lemon, Wright, and Wells heft their medical bags and step back into the chill of the night and return to the station.

It's well after four in the morning now, but the firefighters are wide awake. Their attempts at sleep have been cut short too often to allow them to achieve the deep slumber that the truckies are now enjoying, and their bodies have caught a second wind. But after a few words of light conversation, Lemon, Wright, and Wells make their way back to their beds to give it another try. The rest of the evening passes quietly. Both crews, as well as the people sleeping in the houses that spread out in all directions from Station 14, are lucky enough to pass the last couple of hours before dawn without any more interruption from the sirens.

The rookies, eleven of them, stood lined up with their backs to the rear wall of the P.W. Currie Conference Center on the outskirts of downtown Minneapolis. Dressed in their dark blue, short-sleeved uniform shirts, shiny new badges affixed proudly to their left breasts, they kidded with one another and rocked back and forth in their well-shined black shoes, appearing more anxious than nervous as their beaming friends and relatives slowly filtered in to take their seats. All the top department brass, along with several members of the city council, were on hand to witness the introduction and graduation of the November 2002 class. Chief Rocco Forté mingled amiably with the guests seated on the outer edges of the room, while a slide show of photos showing the rookies working hard in the classroom and at the training tower flickered silently on a projection screen at the front of the room.

The hard, physically demanding work the rookies put in over the past five months was evident in their bare forearms. Many of them stood with their hands clasped in front of them, and the lean muscles that stretched from their wrists to their elbows rippled as they flexed their fingers together. The room where the graduation was held is connected to the city's maintenance facility, and every so often one of the city's big red fire rigs rumbled past the windows that look out onto the street, drawing long stares from the rookies.

The small square room was finally filled to standing room only, and Chief Forté gave the signal that it was time to begin. The rookies filed forward along the side of the room past a long table with bright red paper tablecloths displaying trays of cookies and juice to be consumed after the ceremony, then seated themselves in two short rows of chairs near the front. As they waited for things to get started, the rookies — nine men and two women — continued to chat quietly, drawing a sense of calm from each other and the bonds of camaraderie they had formed over the past five months together. The cheerful interplay helped distract them from the intense and culminant anticipation flowing through their veins.

Once Chief Forté had welcomed everyone, Deputy Chief Jim Clack took the podium and elicited a series of impressed murmurs from his audience as he distributed several honorable service awards to some of the department's veteran crews for their work over the past several months. They included an instance of swift high-rise rescue by Ladder 3 and Engines 5 and 7, as well as the resuscitation of an employee in a grocery store where Ladder 2 was shopping for dinner. Also receiving awards were the crews of Engine 8 and Ladder 5. They discovered and rescued a victim who had been handcuffed to a pole in a building on Lake Street that had been set afire and tightly locked.

After a few more short speeches, the rookies were introduced by two of their instructors, Captain Cherie Penn and Captain Jon Chelstrom. After one final pep talk from the Chief, the folks in the audience pressed forward to congratulate and pose for pictures with the city's newest probationary firefighters, Steve Drew and Heidi Elmer among them. A day before their graduation, Drew and Elmer learned they would be assigned to work the A shift at Station 14. Elmer would start out on the ladder under Captain Tom Rogalski, and Drew would ride with the engine under the tutelage of Penn, who would be heading back to the station now that the current crop of rookies was trained and ready to go.

There are several families that can claim more than one of their own as members of the Minneapolis Fire Department. Firefighting is an inheritance for some, as sons and daughters who grow up with fathers on the job follow in their footsteps. Siblings on the department are also a common occurrence, as word of the job's many benefits travels quickly through the limbs of the family tree, spurring brothers and sisters to follow in their siblings' footsteps.

Steve Drew did not grow up in a firefighting clan, though his family is fast becoming one. His brother Jeff has been a firefighter for the past three years in Rochester, Minnesota, and his brother Curt is a member of Steve's rookie class. Their father applied to the Minneapolis Fire Department years ago and was offered a job but didn't accept it because the sales work he was doing at the time paid better. The sons knew their father later greatly regretted the decision, so when Curt and Steve got the call that they were up for the next rookie class, neither hesitated for a moment to take it up.

Neither of their parents lived to see Curt and Steve become firefighters, but the fact that they both made it through the department's competitive application process and onto the job at the same time has given the brothers pause to think about the guidance their parents might still be exerting in their lives.

"I kind of feel like they had something to do with me getting this job, helping me from up above, you know?" Steve says.

Perhaps. But the burden of proving himself worthy ultimately fell on Drew's shoulders as he embarked on a gauntlet of written, oral, and physical tests, which he navigated well enough to claim a high ranking on the department's hiring list. At the age of twenty-four and with short-cropped, reddish-blonde hair, Drew is the freshest-faced of the current crop of rookies. But his quick smile reveals a slight chip in one of his front teeth that provides a visual clue to his toughness. In rookie school, Drew quickly established himself as an eager apprentice, particularly when it came to the physical work. On their first day at the training tower some three and a half months into their training, the cadets had to complete a precarious ladder climb in order to continue on. Fail, and you were off the department. Just like that. When volunteers were requested, Steve stepped forward before anyone else.

In full gear, which included an air tank on his back and an axe slung to his hip, Steve was the first to complete the task. With four of his classmates butting up to the base of a forty-foot ladder extended straight up into the air, and another four pulling tightly on ropes tied to and stretched out from the top of the ladder to the ground, Drew proceeded to climb to the top. Then he locked himself in and pulled his hands away from the rungs long enough to shout his name and employee number. But the most challenging moment came next. With the aluminum ladder swaying gently, he had to climb over the top to the other side before proceeding back down to the ground.

The harrowing experience proved too much for the nerves of one of the cadets, who was given four different chances on three separate days to make the climb. On his fourth and final try, the cadet froze as he straddled the top of the ladder. The captains had to put in a call to Ladder 11, which made the twenty-minute drive from downtown Minneapolis to rescue the jangled cadet with their aerial ladder and bucket. The rest of the cadets filed quietly away as their comrade was given oxygen in the back of an ambulance. It was a heartbreaking moment for the other cadets, as they realized one of their newest friends, a fellow in his late twenties who had yearned to become a firefighter for much of his life, was not going to continue on with them. Still, they couldn't help but feel the exercise had served its purpose.

"Later that night I was thinking about it," Drew said, "and I felt bad for the guy, but then I thought about if we were working and he freezes up on a building somewhere working off the ladder. It's kind of a risk for the people he's working with and the people we're trying to save."

Neither can Heidi Elmer claim a particularly rich firefighting bloodline. A native of Madison, Wisconsin, she has one uncle who is a retired captain from her hometown department, but that's it. So, growing up she never really considered the possibility of becoming a firefighter herself. Certainly, she had no aversion to physical exertion, as she competed as a speedskater for much of her young life, but it was her more abstract sensibilities that became her guiding light as she matured into adulthood, and she entered the art program at the University of Minnesota in the Twin Cities in 1994. She emerged with her degree in ceramics and sculpture four years later. During her senior year and immediately thereafter, Elmer worked the kilns at a non-profit ceramics studio on Franklin Avenue — near the campus and, incidentally, just down the street from Fire Station 7.

One day early in January of 2000, Elmer and a friend heard about the upcoming application process while visiting with firefighters at the station. They were also told the department was particularly interested in adding more women to the ranks, and the firefighters at Station 7 encouraged Elmer and her friend to apply. Working in the super-heated, clay-baking ovens at the studio was beginning to wear on Elmer, and when her friend joked that firefighting "can't be any hotter than the job we do now," she was startled to find herself giving the idea serious consideration. Another friend at the clay center knew someone on the department, and she also prompted Elmer to give it a go.

Her first love was still working with pottery, but Elmer was well aware that there are not a lot of stable career paths for an artist to follow. Teaching was an option, but Elmer feared it could ultimately drain her of her creative energies. Firefighting's twenty-four-hour shift schedule, she realized, would allow her to continue to work as an artist on her off days, and the more she thought on the other aspects of the job — the camaraderie, serving the public — the more attractive it became. So she stopped off at the fire station one day before work and picked up an application. The testing began midsummer, and Elmer ended up with a ranking of 117 on the hiring list. The department would begin drawing cadets in order from the top of the list as they were needed, and although Elmer was told she should not be discouraged by her ranking, she was also advised not to quit her other job.

But she was fed up with the heat and tough work she was doing for so little pay at the clay center and quit anyway. She spent her time doing landscaping and teaching for the city park board, and kept her fingers crossed that she would one day soon get the nod from the fire department. In January of 2002, a good year and a half after she began her testing, Elmer learned she would be part of the next rookie class. Her family, once they recovered from their initial astonishment over her drastic career shift, provided all kinds of support as she sweated out the fourteen months she waited to get called up. She also noticed they were suddenly much more interested in her work.

"Oh, they were so proud," Elmer relates with a laugh, "so I asked them, 'Why weren't you this proud when I was an artist?'"

But a city budget cut forced the department to put the new class on hold 10 days before it was scheduled to start. In May, the rookies got another call saying they would start up on June 3, but they had all learned their lesson and would not believe they were in the door until their classes actually started. The starting date rolled around without any delays this time, and the rookies breathed a collective sigh of relief as they came together to begin their training.

They had little time to reflect on their good fortune, however, as they spent their first week, as Steve put it, "getting their asses kicked" by their instructors. They would spend long periods of time chopping on a roof in full gear before class even started one day. The next, they would be ordered to haul massive electrical fans up and down the steps in the six-story training tower. And for the next three and a half months, the rookies were never told what they could expect from day to day. There would be days that were all bookwork or EMS training, others that were physical blowouts, and still others that were a mixture of both. Curt Drew found parts of the training more grueling than what he experienced during his days as a U.S. Marine.

And contrary to the warnings they received at the outset — that there would inevitably be disputes between them as their time together wore on — the classmates hit it off fabulously from the start. They quickly took to hanging out with one another away from their training, and they thrived on each other's support and encouragement when things got tough.

For Elmer and Stephanie Johnson — the other woman in the rookie class — it was also a great relief to find that none of their male classmates had any hang-ups about working with them. Johnson and Elmer's appreciation of their cohorts' egalitarian attitudes grew when, upon meeting up with a group of cadets — all male — from another Twin Cities fire department, some of them seemed ill at ease around the women.

"Maybe these guys in our class are exceptional, but they never had any problem with it, from day one," Elmer said.

Following their graduation, the new rookies were given a week off (forced vacation, some called it) before reporting to their stations. For many, it was the longest week of their lives. Elmer tried to wile away the days by running errands, doing laundry, and ironing her uniform repeatedly. By the time the night before her first day on the job rolled around, every last thread of her uniform was wrinkle-free.

Rookies often spend the night before their first day dreaming about the action they'll see. That is, if they get any sleep at all, and most don't. The anticipation of putting into practice that which they learned in rookie school, coupled with harried situations that will have members of the public and their veteran coworkers counting on them, is an emotional brew that's sure to keep even the drowsiest narcoleptic awake at night. Rookies imagine going to battle with a fully involved burner with flames shooting from the windows of the upper floors of a building. In reality, most of the fires they face in their first few months on the job end up being the usual car fires or quick knockdowns in basements or garages, and the new firefighters soon begin to wonder if the big one is ever going to come. It's about that time that their more seasoned counterparts assure them that things seemed a little slow when they were rookies, too. Relax, the vets will say, sooner or later they'll find themselves in a real dogfight with the red devil.

The veterans might also inform them that, despite all their preparation and all the outstanding resources at their disposal, and even with all the mental role-playing they go through, when it comes time to make their first aggressive interior attack, time will trip into a sort of hyperspeed mode. They'll barely comprehend what is happening, even in the immediate few feet around them, and they'll do well just to stay close to their captain.

Neither Drew nor Elmer got much rest last night. Elmer spent the eve of her fire career taking in a Peter Gabriel concert in downtown Minneapolis, where she was able to expend some of her nervous energy. Now the mid-November sun is rising beyond the horizon to the east as they arrive bright and early at Station 14. It's Saturday — cleaning day — and after getting their gear situated in the rigs and checking in with the captains, both leap into action scrubbing down the station with the other firefighters — Penn, Jay Wells, and Mark Hilton on Engine 14; and Rogalski, Shawn Modahl, and Bob Niznik on Ladder 10. Most of the cleaning chores are completed by midmorning, and the veteran firefighters spread out around the station. Elmer and Drew, meanwhile, still have their heads down and are scrubbing and sweeping dust off their respective rigs.

Rogalski informs Elmer that he'd like her to put a fresh coat of paint on one of the ladder truck's axes at some point during the day. He then pulls up a chair alongside Modahl and Hilton in the dining room, where they all read the morning paper. About twenty minutes later, Elmer enters through the kitchen, drying her hands with a towel.

"Is there anything else I can do for you?" she asks Rogalski, who looks up from his paper.

"No, I don't think so."

"Okay," Elmer says. "Are you sure? Is there anything I can clean for you?"

"Nope. Well, did you paint that axe?"

"Yep, it's all done."

"Okay, then no, that's good for now."

"Okay," Elmer says, then wheels away and heads back through the kitchen towards the apparatus floor.

Rogalski and Modahl look at each other and grin at the rookie's industriousness. The captain looks at his watch. It's just after ten-thirty.

"You've got to learn to pace yourself, kid!" Rogalski playfully shouts after Elmer.

The rookies know their new colleagues are observing them, and they are eager to please their superiors while proving to the other firefighters that they will work hard and have what it takes to do the job right. Not only will they have to prove they can work effectively on the fireground or at a medical scene, but also that they can be counted on to carry their weight around the firehouse, whether it be cleaning the equipment, scrubbing the toilets, or cooking food for the clutch. But so much of the job is made up of the social aspects of station life that rookies also have to learn when it's appropriate to throttle back a bit and relax. Rogalski appreciates the fact that Elmer is displaying a willingness to work, but he also wants his rookie to understand that she isn't required to consume herself with busywork just in order to impress him on the first day. There is a lot to learn, and there are always things that can be done around the station, but setting the right pace to the day is an important facet of firehouse life. It's a long shift, after all.

Elmer and Drew continue to hover quietly around the rigs and the workbench, touching up paint on the tools and keeping things as spotless as they can. They are also waiting for those alarm tones to ring out, as the sun has climbed high into the sky to illuminate a gorgeous autumn day, and they are anxious to see some action.

At forty-one minutes after one in the afternoon, the speakers finally blare. A run for Engine 14 sends Drew and his crewmates scurrying for the rig, and Wells has them quickly out the door. Drew's first medical run with the Minneapolis Fire Department is not particularly dramatic, though, and they return home in a matter of minutes.

Shortly before noon, Rogalski instructs his company to saddle up; it's the ladder crew's turn to check vacants this week. As the big rig snakes its way through the streets, Rogalski points out various vacant houses the department needs to be particularly aware of, and Elmer drinks it all in. Rogalski points to a small, squat house with plywood on all the windows, then twists around toward Elmer.

"That house has a basement that's been all carved up into small rooms, Heidi," Rogalski relates as the rookie nods attentively. "It could be very disorienting if there's a fire in there. And if we had a basement fire there, we are going to have to ventilate right away, because there's only one small staircase down into the basement, and those guys who are taking the tank line in are going to take a shit-kicking, because there's only one place for that heat and smoke to go, and that's right up the stairs."

The next vacant they come to, Rogalski has his rookie do a quick walk-around to see that the doors and windows are still securely closed up. She returns about a minute later and says a piece of plywood over one of the windows is missing a couple of screws but is still on nice and tight. Satisfied, Rogalski nods for Modahl to steer the rig to the next address. After they've completed their list, the ladder crew makes a stop at the grocery store, and Niznik jumps down from the till and heads in to buy food. He's cooking tonight.

"Heidi, you might want to go in and shop with him so you can get an idea about how much food you'll have to buy when you cook," Rogalski says, and the rookie bounds from the truck and jogs to catch up with Niznik. After they return with teeming shopping bags in each hand, and after a quick stop at Subway to grab lunch, Ladder 10 returns to the station and chows down.

After they finish eating, Rogalski has Modahl and Niznik pull the truck out onto the driveway. Ladder 10's regular rig is in the shop for repairs, and the twenty-four-year-old replacement rig's generator is acting up. Rogalski wants to get it out into the open air before they fire it up and let it run to make sure it's reliable. Without it, the ladder can't operate a lot of its power equipment.

At five after two, Elmer is going over her ops manual in the coop when the outside bell rings, then BEEP BEEP BEEP BEEP BEEP, the steady cadence for a fire alarm echoes through the station. Elmer stands up from her chair and freezes for just a moment, unsure of whether the call is for Ladder 10 or just Engine 14. Then she sees Modahl and Niznik running for the front door with Rogalski walking swiftly behind them, and she quickly gives chase.

Because the ladder truck is parked outside, Elmer has to grab her boots off the apparatus floor and kicks her shoes off before rushing to the step up into her seat on the rig. She pulls her boots and bunker pants on quickly. Before the day had started, Elmer had determined to make it into her seat before her driver and her captain on her first run, but seeing that Modahl and Rogalski are already climbing into the rig, she throws her jacket up into her seat and pulls herself up. Drew and the rest of Engine 14 pull through their door and set off to the south on James, sirens crying. Modahl has Ladder 10 on the road moments later, sirens wailing, air horn booming.

Elmer fastens her coat and slides into the straps of her air tank before pulling on her hood and helmet and checking to make sure her other crucial equipment is in place. It takes more than a minute for Modahl to steer Ladder 10 to the scene, but time flashes by so quickly that Elmer is shocked when she looks out her window to see that they've arrived. It feels to her like they just set out from the station a few seconds ago. Time warped forward on her as she ran through her mental checklist.

As the ladder crew begins grabbing its tools, Penn makes her way around to the back of the house. Smoke is billowing out from the back door, and she masks up and plunges in to the thick flood of smoke boiling up from staircase leading into the basement. Drew and Hilton begin pulling a line from the hose bed as Wells gets the pump revved up. Rogalski tells Elmer to grab a pump can, and Modahl and Niznik detach axes and hooks from the ladder truck. The ladder crew makes its way to the back of the house just as Penn reappears through the back door. She informs Rogalski that it's a basement fire, and he turns and instructs Modahl and Niznik to begin ventilating the basement floor windows. The duo disappears back around the corner. Drew and Hilton have the line stretched, and the rookie is waiting with the nozzle just outside the back door. Penn instructs him to hold tight just outside the door and be ready to come in at a moment's notice.

"Okay, Heidi, we're going in," Rogalski says. "Mask up, and leave your flashlight off when you follow me in so that it doesn't interfere with me while I look for the fire."

Rogalski expertly pulls his air mask into place over his head and re-secures his helmet. Elmer begins to do the same, but for some reason she can't get her mask all the way to her face.

Realizing that her captain is ready and watching her, she sees that the air tube that leads from her mask to her air tank is tangled around her shoulder strap. She quickly loosens the strap and begins unwinding the tube, but a feeling of dread seeps into her body as she realizes Rogalski has picked up the pump can and is ready to head back into the house behind Penn. No, no, no, Elmer thinks, it's her first fire and the pump can is her one responsibility, and now her captain has snatched it up. Once her mask is freed and in place, she bounds up the steps and falls in behind her captain, who has turned to see if she is with him.

Elmer seizes the opportunity to get her weapon back: "Can I have the pump can?" Rogalski hands it to her, then leads Elmer into the house.

Immediately upon entering the door, they turn to their right and begin walking down a staircase that is filled with opaque black smoke. It is darker and seems more sinister than the lighter vegetable-oil smoke the rookies trained with at the tower. The only thing Elmer can see as she descends through the thick haze is the reflective tape on her captain's coat. When she reaches the bottom of the staircase, Elmer turns and can see an orange glow through the smoke. Niznik and Modahl have gotten the windows opened up, so the smoke is beginning to thin out, just enough for the captains and Elmer to make their way over without being completely blind.

Rogalski turns to Elmer.

"See it?" he asks through the thick plastic of his mask.

"Yeah," Elmer replies as she pulls her gloves on and walks over toward the glow. Elmer is not sure what is burning, but it looks somehow artificial, kind of like the undulating flames in one of those fake fireplaces.

"Get the pump can on it," Rogalski says, then turns to help get another of the windows opened. Elmer unravels the small hose and grabs the handle, ready to pump. Unsure if she should wait until Rogalski gets the window open in case the water hitting the flame causes another cloud of blinding smoke, she steps back toward him and taps him on the shoulder. He turns.

"Water?" she asks simply.

"Yeah," Rogalski says.

Elmer churns the pump handle up and down, and the water pours forth, unleashing smoke and gurgling steam as the fire flags, then finally goes out. Modahl and Niznik have pulled two massive fans off the bed of the ladder truck and have hung them in a window and a door to help suck the rest of the smoke from the house. They then return to the basement, where the others are looking at the cause of the fire — a burning candle that melted down into the top of a large television on which it was sitting. The truckies haul the ruined TV, which has melted in on itself almost beyond the point of recognition, out into the backyard and set it in front of two young men who were in the house when the fire started. They gawk silently at the remains.

Back in the thinning haze of the basement, Rogalski and Penn continue to search the wall near where the TV was sitting to make sure the fire did not extend into it. The wall is scorched, but the captains can find no evidence that the fire is still lurking inside somewhere, waiting to break out again later. The smoke has smirched thousands of strands of spider webs on the ceiling, and they now dangle gently as a sea of dark gossamer threads above the heads of the firefighters. Luckily for the home's owners, the department's quick response kept the flames from spreading, and the captains point out to the rookies all of the nearby spots where fire could have gotten into the walls. There are also several blankets hanging on a wall several feet away that would have gone up quickly had the flames reached them. The only significant damage came in the form of the smoke that permeated the basement and parts of the first floor. The TV, of course, is ruined. The pipes and other drug paraphernalia sitting on a table next to where the fire started appear to have gone unscathed.

The captains and rookies make their way back up the steps and out the back door. The two young men watch the firefighters sheepishly. They must know that their drugs were sitting in plain view of the firefighters after they extinguished the flames, and they are no doubt wondering whether they are about to be busted. But the firefighters say nothing and simply file around the corner toward the street.

Back out in front, Drew helps repack the tank line back onto the hose bed while Elmer and the truckies return their tools to their rightful places. With everything back in place, the rookies meet on the sidewalk and speak quietly, but excitedly, comparing notes over what just took place. Niznik walks past and smiles broadly at their enthusiasm.

"They're loving this," he says.

On the way back to the station, Rogalski turns and asks Elmer if she has any questions about what just went on. She says no, and Rogalski tells her one of the best things she can do early on at a fire is to relax and make sure she has all her equipment in order, so that little holdups like the tangled mask don't occur again.

"But you did a good job," he tells her, and Elmer smiles.

At the station, Elmer refills the pump can with water and places it back on the rig. Another alarm comes in and both rigs are soon back out the door in search of an outside fire, but it turns out to be a small authorized burn in someone's yard.

As evening begins to approach, Niznik sets to work preparing the evening's dinner. Two massive pots on the stove are soon filled with boiling noodles and chicken breasts drowning in a red sauce. The rookies help set the table, and Niznik is putting the final touches on the meal when the alarm bell rings. Another fire, this time an alley garage on Morgan. Niznik shuts down the stove and rushes to join the others as they clamber into the rigs.

Engine 14 spots the smoke and pulls down the alley near the burning structure, while Ladder 10 takes up a position on the street just to the south. The flames have already blackened one entire corner of the large boxy garage, and the aluminum siding has melted, the individual slats now drooping like large strips of warm taffy. Smoke seeps heavily from beneath the overhang of the roof.

Rogalski and Niznik begin hacking with their axes at a tall wooden fence that separates the alley from the backyard and butts up against the burning section of garage. People from neighboring houses have started to appear in the alley, jackets pulled tight against the chill of the deep autumn evening. A middle-aged man wearing a green robe and slippers walks to the alley from the house in front of the garage. Soon, some of the women in the neighboring yard begin arguing loudly. Someone nearby says something about someone pouring hot ashes on a compost heap, but the firefighters are too busy working on extinguishing the flames to sort out exactly what is going on.

The wooden fence now chopped away, Rogalski walks through and plays his flashlight around the area. There is indeed a compost heap along the edge of the garage that borders a neighbor's yard. Penn has had her crew pull a short length of hose from Engine 14's tank, and she has Drew open up the line to kill the flames and cool the outer edge of the garage and the underside of the roof. The water splatters off the garage and back to the paved alley like a heavy rain. Modahl and Niznik then move in with hooks and begin pulling the siding off, and Drew follows with another spraying. A visibly shaken woman appears from the yard and rushes past the firefighters and disappears into the house next door. More shouting.

Penn and Rogalski ask the man in the robe to open the garage so they can look inside. The fire has not reached too far into the interior and seems to be out, but the captains are concerned that there is still a significant amount of smoke bleeding through the top of the structure. So Rogalski has Niznik and Modahl use their hooks to pull away at several feet of the gutter and soffitt to see if the fire is hiding underneath it. After a good five minutes of this, Drew gives the whole area another quick washing-down, and the captains are satisfied that the fire is out.

As the crews pack up, two neighbor women are talking pleasantly near another garage. One asks the other if she is the one who called the fire department.

"Yeah, and they really got here fast. I couldn't believe it," the other says, then adds with a boisterous laugh, "Now I know when I need the police in a hurry I can just call the fire department."

Back on the truck, Rogalski, a long smear of black soot on one side of his neck, turns his attention to Elmer.

"Did you hear those people screaming at each other?" he asks, and she says yes. The captain continues. "Man, sometimes people just go nuts. I'm not kidding you, I've gone to fires where people are fist-fighting right in the front yard and we're laying a tank line right past them. If you ever see that, just worry about doing your job, and if you need the police, just call a squad. We have a very good working relationship with the police, and when we call them, they're there."

"Awesome," comes Elmer's reply.

Rogalski goes on to explain to the rookie his reasons for having his crew continue to open the upper reaches of the roof, even after no more flame was visible.

"I saw the gutter still smoking and I thought, 'If we don't get that down, we'll be here again later.' But instead, we took ten extra minutes and pulled that all down, and now I'm one hundred percent sure we won't be coming back here tonight."

As the drivers back the rigs into place, Penn pulls the door to the coop open. She jumps back and lets out a high-pitched, blood-curdling scream. The other firefighters' heads snap around in her direction, but Penn, after a moment frozen in her tracks, doubles over with a mixture of relief and laughter.

"When I opened the door, that leaf came blowing out," she says, pointing to the floor. "I thought it was a mouse."

The others smile, as they know Penn — the tough disciplinarian and assertive fire commander — is afraid of mice, and more and more of the rodents have been spotted on the apparatus floor and elsewhere in the station since the temperatures outside have started dropping. Someone points out to Penn that she needn't worry, as several boxes filled with tiny blue pellets of mouse poison have been set out around the station.

"Are you kidding?" she retorts. "That stuff is just little blue cookies to them."

Niznik heads back into the kitchen to see if the dinner he prepared is still salvageable. It is, but the noodles have become mushy from sitting in the pan of hot water while they were at the fire.

"I usually have a tendency to undercook them. This time they're overcooked," he says, then smiles his broad, toothy smile and shrugs. "You can't win."

But the firefighters are hungry after the two skirmishes they've been involved in since lunch, and no one says a word about the noodles as they wolf down the food. The rookies are quiet during dinner, content to listen in on the light conversation floating between the veterans.

"Shawn, did you ever get the chance to work at Tens?" Niznik asks Modahl, referring to Station 10 located downtown on North Fourth Street. The station closed its doors last year after providing the city with ninety-eight years and nine months of service.

"Oh yeah," Modahl replies.

"How about you, Tom?"

"I was stationed there for the last year it was open." Rogalski says.

The old fire station, which used to house horse-drawn companies and was later home to the city's first motorized apparatus, is now occupied by the police department. The firefighters who got the chance to work in the station loved it. Embedded in the heart of the city's club and nightlife district between Hennepin and First Avenues, the pedestrian traffic outside the station always made for great people-watching.

"You never got to bed before two o'clock when it was Friday or Saturday night, but you never really wanted to, because you wanted to watch the show," Rogalski says.

"I tried to swap shifts three different times, just so I could say I worked there at least one day," Hilton says, "and all three times I got tramped out somewhere else."

Nearly every firefighter who worked at Station 10 for any length of time has some crazy story to tell. Jackson Millikan vividly recalls his first day as a rookie at the station. It was Christmas Day 1999, and shortly after Millikan checked in, a man bleeding from the neck wandered in from a nearby bar. After a night at the bar, he had gotten into a fight with another man, who stabbed him in the throat. Millikan and the other firefighters did their best to stop the flow of blood until the ambulance arrived to take the man to the hospital. Bleeding night owls wandering into Station 10 were not an uncommon occurrence.

The station was closed because the department determined that other stations that have been built in and around the city's core over the years, including Stations 1 and Station 6 right downtown, are sufficient to cover that part of the city. But the firefighters already miss it.

"I was driving by it the other day with my wife and I told her it's such a shame to see it sitting there without any rigs in it,"

Rogalski says, and everyone turns their attention back to their food. A hockey game is playing on the TV on top of the refrigerator. "We never get to watch TV, this is kind of nice," says Niznik, who is only filling in at Station 14 today. Station 11 is his usual home. "Declouet always turns on the jazz station over the intercom and we have to listen to that."

"Geez, what do you guys do, put candles out and turn the lights down, too?" Modahl ribs, and the others chuckle.

Penn, who rarely goes in on the evening meal, shows up through the door and addresses the rookies.

"Do you guys have any questions?" she asks, and they wag their heads no.

"A little bit later we'll go out and go over the engine top to bottom for your school tonight," she says. "You know where to find me; I'll be up in my office doing some paperwork. These guys will take good care of you. They'll teach you how to wash dishes."

The crews polish off their meal, and the rookies spring to their feet and set to clearing the table. The chairs are rolled into the garage and the tables scooted to the wall, and Drew has just begun mopping the floor when Engine 14 is called out for a small child having trouble breathing. They're back quickly, and Drew goes right back to his mop while Elmer and the other truckies get the kitchen cleaned up and the dishwasher started.

The remainder of Drew and Elmer's first day on the job is relatively quiet — a few quick medical runs for the engine, and a good night's sleep for the ladder crew. But two shifts later, Drew gets his first taste of violence when Engine 14 is called to a shooting at a nearby residence.

Inside they find a man in his late teens who has been shot twice at point-blank range and is lying on the floor. He is conscious, but scared and in a lot of pain. A young woman tells the firefighters he got into a fight with another man — over her, apparently — and the other guy pulled out a gun and leveled two shots into the stricken man's upper body from a few inches away. He's lucky. One shot went through the man's sternum, the other through his shoulder. Both bullets exited his back without killing him. Penn and Dan Schultz work to get the flow of blood stopped while Drew applies oxygen. Penn notices that Drew's hands are trembling just a bit. Good, she thinks, his adrenaline's going.

Soon the paramedics arrive and the man is placed on the stretcher. He is being lifted into the ambulance, and Drew climbs in to set up an IV for his arm. The last thing the firefighters hear before the doors are closed is the young man's pleas for assurance from the paramedics.

"Am I gonna make it?" he asks, his voice riddled with fear. "Am I gonna make it?"

Back at the station, Schultz shows Drew how to disinfect the medical gear following a bloody scene like this one. A short time later, while seated in one of the old couches in the upstairs locker room, Drew reflects on his first few days on the job. His training, he says, has kicked in and guided him in every situation so far, and it allowed him to stay calm and aware at the shooting scene, even though his body was coursing with exhilaration. He is already itching for the bell to ring again so he can go back to work.

"I'm just waiting for that big fire, flames shooting out the windows, and hopefully I'm on the nozzle," he says. "But I'm just thinking about how my brother in Rochester might never even see a shooting on the job, and here I've already been to one on my third day."

ANSWERING THE BELL

Drew and Wright bound from the cab of Engine 14 and sprint toward the steps of a small, aging apartment building on Golden Valley Road, where a woman stands waving to them. They have medical bags and equipment in hand and slung over their shoulders as they rush up the sidewalk, while Caouette gets the rig parked and Penn acknowledges to dispatch that they have arrived on scene.

The call came in for "one unconscious," and the dispatcher updated the crew that the victim might be in full cardiac arrest when they were two blocks away. The girl at the door has her coat pulled tight against the frigid air of this mid-December night. As Wright and Drew reach her, the girl tells them, very calmly, "She's laying upstairs with no pulse and she's not breathing."

This is bad news, yet Wright is struck by just how unruffled the girl seems by the words she has just spoken.

"What apartment?" Wright demands.

"202."

Penn and Caouette have caught up by now, and all four firefighters hurry through the door and up the stairway to the apartment. It's dimly lit as they enter, but they can see a woman lying on her back in an interior doorway and rush to her side.

181

There are three other women in the apartment and, much like the girl at the door, they seem too tranquil somehow. After all, there is a woman — someone they certainly must know — lying completely motionless on the floor in front of them. But they are as calm as if the firefighters who just entered the apartment are the mailman delivering a package. One is even leisurely puffing on a cigarette.

"Let's move her out into the hall where we can see her," Wright says, then moves toward the woman's head as Drew grabs her bare feet and looks up in astonishment.

"Her feet are cold," he says.

They slide the tiny woman, who appears to be in her forties, into the hall, but the light is still not good enough, and Penn instructs them to move her again — around the corner into the living room and underneath a light on the wall where they can see what they're doing. The firefighters drop to the ground and prepare to go to work. Penn goes straight for the woman's wrists to check for a pulse. Nothing. The woman's flesh is cold and her hands are curled into tight little claws. Her palms are purple. From there, Penn checks for a carotid pulse on the neck. Again, nothing, and she knows the woman is in big trouble, probably beyond all help.

"Get the AED ready," Penn says, referring to the portable heart-start machine they have brought with them. "Get the scissors. Get the scissors."

Caouette grabs the scissors from one of the bags and quickly tears through the front of the woman's T-shirt and pulls it back. The woman has no bra to clip open. She is showing no signs of life, and Caouette rocks the woman slightly on to her side to check for the gravitational pooling of blood on her back. Nothing yet. Penn begins asking the other women in the room questions. Their answers come back vague, uncertain, and generally unhelpful. One of the women says the victim is her sister, but no one seems to know her name or how old she is. One says she's thirty-seven, maybe thirty-nine, they're not sure.

"When's the last time you saw her up and around?" Penn asks.

"Five, ten minutes ago," one of the women says, which seems

hard to believe. The woman's body is much too cold, and the firefighters can't imagine that she could have lost so much body heat in such a short period of time, especially when they consider that the apartment seems to be well-heated.

"What's her past medical history?" Penn asks.

"She's got asthma."

"Is she taking any medication for her asthma?"

"I think she's taking something, but I don't know what."

Penn asks again if they're sure they saw her just five to ten minutes ago. They say yes. Sometimes firefighters get a feeling in their gut that things just aren't right with the situation, and Penn is getting that feeling now.

"Has she been doing anything tonight, any drugs, any drinking?" Penn continues as Wright tries to get a breathing tube into the woman's nose, to no avail. Her nostrils are too tight. He already tried to insert a tube through her mouth, but her jaw muscles are clenched tight as a vice.

"She had a cigarette," one of the women says.

"Has she been sick?"

"Don't know."

Caouette attaches the AED pads to the upper-right and lower-left corners of the woman's torso, and she and Penn set up the mechanical resuscitator that will try to breathe for the woman. The AED gives medical responders visual and audio cues, and it now instructs the firefighters to stand clear as it attempts to detect how the woman's heart is working, if at all. If the heart is quivering out of its usual rhythm, the unit will send a jolt of electricity through the pads in an attempt to get the heart back in step. The unit's mechanical voice indicates it cannot detect anything, though, and it instructs the firefighters to check again for a pulse, and to start CPR if they can't find one.

"Get her head straightened out," Penn says. As Wright prepares to inject air into the woman's lungs, Drew moves into position to begin compressions on the woman's chest. Caouette asks the woman who is smoking to put out her cigarette. She does.

Wright pushes the button on the resuscitator and sends a surge of air in through the woman's mouth. Drew begins his compressions. With the first thrust of his palms into the woman's sternum, he feels the tendons in her rib cage crackle in resistance, a good sign that he's applying the right amount of pressure. After five compressions, Wright hits the button and sends another burst of air into the woman's mouth. The woman's chest heaves a bit as it inflates artificially.

They repeat this a couple of times and the woman begins to gurgle. Wright reflexively rolls from his knees back up onto his heels. He's heard that sound before when performing CPR, and he knows the woman could be about to vomit. If the woman's lungs are not taking the air, it could be shunted into her stomach, and any food or drink she's had will likely come spewing back up. It's a lesson Wright learned the hard way early in his career, so he's repositioned himself to be able to get out of the way quickly, if need be.

Drew seems unaware of the possibility that he could soon be the target of projectile vomit and is still on his knees and hunched over the woman's torso as he performs compressions. The safety goggles that would protect his eyes from any fluid dangle loosely around his neck. Penn notices this, and also sees that the rookie's adrenaline is rushing to the point that it's now causing him to perform the chest compressions at too rapid a pace.

Penn knows this is Drew's first time performing CPR under live-fire conditions, so she moves to his side, bends down, and speaks softly but firmly to him. Slow it down a little. You're doing fine. Just slow it down a little. The captain's hand is on Drew's back, a calming gesture. And now she begins pushing gently with her hand to give Drew a steady pace to follow as he makes his compressions. Penn counts: a thousand one, a thousand two, a thousand three. She wants to reassure Drew that he's doing okay, but without making a scene out of it. Had she simply barked at him to slow down, it might give the impression that he doesn't know what he's doing to the other women in the room, which could aggravate the situation. Penn was one of Drew's training captains, so she knows he's got what it takes. He just needs the experience. You can practice perfectly on a medical dummy all you want in rookie school, but there's no substitute for the real

184

thing when it comes to learning how to keep your adrenaline in check.

The paramedics have arrived and are preparing their EKG to test the activity of the woman's heart. Penn fills them in on what she knows about the victim, which isn't much — they still don't even have her name — and the paramedics begin asking the other women many of the same questions. They get many of the same fuzzy answers. Penn takes it all in as she watches her firefighters assist the paramedics with their equipment and procedures. Things just seem too fishy. And the fact that they claim to have seen the victim up and moving about so recently continues to gnaw at her. The woman was ice cold when they arrived, suggesting that she had been down, and possibly dead, for some time before anyone even called 911.

Penn makes her decision and moves to Caouette's side and speaks quietly into her ear.

"I'm going to request the police, so I'm going to step around the corner if you need me."

As Penn begins to move away, she sees that the paramedics' heart monitor is flatlining — still no heartbeat, still no sign of any life at all.

In the hallway, Penn cues her radio.

"Dispatch, Engine 14, I'm requesting a squad, code two, for a possibly suspicious DOA."

"Received."

As Penn re-enters the apartment, another woman who has just arrived follows her through the doorway. The firefighters and paramedics are standing, inactive for the most part, around the woman on the floor.

The newly arrived woman is agitated. She asks: "What are you doing? Aren't you going to try to work on her?"

One of the paramedics turns toward her and, after a brief pause, utters "No, I'm sorry. She's passed."

The woman begins crying, and one of the other women tries to console her. The other women in the room still don't seem at all rattled. One of them makes a cell phone call. Another lights up a cigarette.

185

Caouette gets up and finds a towel and drapes it over the woman's torso and head. Penn then asks her to go down and open the door to let the police in. Caouette exits the apartment, and she is startled to see three cops sprinting up the steps past her into the apartment. Penn sees them rush through the door and is concerned that the sudden appearance of the police in the apartment might inflame the women. They have been acting so oddly since the moment the firefighters arrived that she feels the situation is unpredictable, so she backs the cops back out into the hallway.

"What's going on?" she asks.

"They said you guys needed help," one of the officers says.

"I never said that," Penn replies. "It's just a suspicious DOA."

Apparently the dispatcher believed the firefighters were in some sort of danger when Penn made her call for the squad, which explains their hurried entrance to the scene.

"What makes it suspicious?" the cop asks.

Penn explains the situation and how the women inside have been acting. The officer explains that they didn't know what they were getting into when they received the call from dispatch, which is why they came so quickly and with backup. Her concerns about the potential volatility of the situation notwithstanding, Penn is grateful the police rushed to their side so quickly.

Penn is even more thankful for the officers' presence when other relatives of the deceased woman begin showing up. An older man comes in from the outside and tries frantically to make his way to the apartment, shouting "That's my daughter! That's my daughter!" But the police have decided the apartment is a possible crime scene, and thus can't allow anyone to enter. So they stop the man at the steps and ask him to please calm down and wait here. Penn, who has returned to the apartment with one of the officers, can hear the man's shouts as they echo through the outer hallways.

Soon, two more men, younger than the first, arrive and add to the din as they try to get to the apartment.

"That's my sister! That's my mother-fucking sister in there!" one of them shouts over and over, but the police keep them back, too.

The women in the apartment are being held there, and they too begin to become agitated. What's going on? Why are the police here? Why won't you let her family in?

Penn tries to calm the women.

"The deal is," she explains, "we've all got a job to do here, and the cops are not trying to do anything to further upset you or further complicate a bad situation. But they have protocol they need to follow, and letting people in here will violate their protocol. Please just let us do our jobs, okay?"

The women are not happy, but they seem to accept Penn's assurances. As more officers arrive and begin separating the women to different rooms of the apartment, Penn has her crew pack up the equipment and prepare to move out. They can do no more here, and the small apartment is quickly filling up with cops. Everything accounted for, the firefighters file past the police manning the steps and out the door, where there are eight squad cars now parked, lights flashing, near the front of the building. The usual crowd has gathered, and the firefighters make their way through it and back to their rig.

As Caouette steers the fire engine back into the flow of traffic, Drew is the first to speak.

"Cherie, why did you consider that scene suspicious?"

Pleased by the rookie's inquisitiveness, the captain explains the factors that compelled her to make the call. Wright and Caouette, who have also seen their share of emergency medical scenes, agree that things didn't seem quite right, and they thank their captain for her leadership and calming influence. Shortly after they arrive back at the station, Penn receives a call from the police that they would like the fire crew to return to the scene and speak to a homicide investigator. They do so, and the investigator takes down the names and contact information for all of the firefighters for his records. After a minute or so of small talk with the police officers still on scene, the firefighters head back to their station again.

Penn calls her crew together and lets them know they might want to jot down all the details they can remember from the scene, in case the police investigators have any questions for them in the future. If the cops do indeed find the woman's death to be the result of foul play, they might want to know if the firefighters have any information that can shed light onto their investigation — if they saw or heard anything unusual.

Before they spread out into the station, the Engine 14 crew hangs out for a few minutes more in the coop, discussing the way they handled the scene. Then someone changes the subject and they begin joking around, and before long they are laughing uproariously. Their hilarity roars loudly off the walls in the tiny room, so loudly in fact that Penn reaches over to close the door leading into the TV room, where a couple of the truckies are watching a movie.

Drew seems particularly grateful for the levity, and he chuckles hard at the joking of Penn and Caouette. A few minutes ago, when the crew had just returned to the station for the second time, the rookie seemed a bit subdued as he leaned against the back of the fire engine, holding his navy blue uniform cap in one hand and rubbing the other across the short stubble on his scalp. He had just returned from trying unsuccessfully to revive a dead woman less than a month after his first day on the job, and it seemed to be weighing on him a bit. The laughter of his veteran crewmates is a clear and unmistakable signal to the rookie that it's okay to move on — that he has to move on, right now — to put the death behind him, and get on with life as a firefighter in a big city.

It's next shift and the day is unusually quiet again — a single medical call early in the day is all the firefighters at Station 14 have responded to as the dinner hour approaches. The sun is setting somewhere behind the gray lid of clouds that cloaks the entire city, and the ashen light of another wintry day is weakening by the minute. The Christmas lights strung across trees and fences of nearby houses wink to life.

The bell rings. The call is for Engine 14 to a possible shooting. Modahl is driving today, and he and Penn hop aboard as Schultz and Elmer climb in behind them. Modahl steers the rig south on James and heads east on Lowry for a few blocks before pulling to the side of the road. Penn informs dispatch they are staging a block away from the scene. The police have the scene secured a minute later, and Modahl urges the fire engine around the corner and another block south, finally parking it near the entrance of an alley where police and several other people are waving to them.

The firefighters hustle into the throat of the alley and come to a stop near a man who's lying on his back near a pair of large plastic garbage cans. The wind is kicking up, and small swirls of snow are eddying like tiny galaxies around the man's prostrate form. He seems to be in his mid-twenties and is wearing jeans and a winter coat, unzipped and exposing a white T-shirt that is sopped with bright red blood on one side. The firefighters go to work.

"Okay, get him out of this," Penn says, "Sir, we're going to lift you up a little bit and get your coat off. I need a flashlight; can we get a light?"

One of the cops trains a flashlight on the man as the others begin moving bystanders back from the scene.

"There it is," Elmer says. She is kneeling near the man's head and has pulled his shirt up to his chest. Blood is running out of two small holes on the right side of the man's rib cage and belly.

"All right, lay him back down and get the O-two on him," Penn commands. Modahl readies the oxygen bottle as Schultz pulls a few patches of thick gauze from the medical bag and hands them to Penn, who applies them to the man's wounds.

"I'm going to put this on you to help you breathe, okay? It'll help you breathe," Elmer says to the man as she straps the oxygen mask over his mouth and nose. He has yet to speak a word in reply, and he is having a hard time keeping his eyes open for more than a second or two at a time.

A man who looks a little older than the victim is standing about ten feet away and begins shouting to his fallen friend.

"Talk, man, talk!...C'mon man, talk!"

Penn turns to the man: "What's his name?"

"Kunta."

"Kunta, listen to me, tell me if this hurts," Penn says as she prods the area around his wounds. Kunta shakes his head. "No? What about here?"

He manages to rasp out a "no" through the oxygen mask.

The dispatcher's voice comes over the radio in Penn's hand:

"Engine 14, checking to see if your victim is a stomach injury."

"Affirmative," Penn replies.

The bullet holes on the right side appear to be entry wounds, and Modahl and Elmer are searching Kunta's torso for possible exit holes.

"You guys got bullet holes on both sides?" Penn asks.

"Yep."

"I need another five by nine. Someone get vitals on him."

Schultz digs back in for more gauze as Modahl straps the blood-pressure cuff to the man's arm. More and more police are arriving on the scene, but there is no ambulance yet. Some of the cops have been asking people if they saw anything.

"Have we got any information yet?" Penn asks one of the officers. Kunta lets out a loud moan before the cop can answer. Kunta's eyes are fluttering, and Penn tries to keep his mental faculties engaged: "Kunta, how you doing? Stay with us. Stay with us. Kunta! How you doing? How you doing?"

As the firefighters continue to work on Kunta, another man standing nearby with a cell phone in his hand yells to a cop: "Someone shot my friend!"

"Sir, they're working on him. Please stay back."

The man grows louder and indignant: "My friend, man, someone shot my friend! He's down on Fremont!"

The cop pauses for a moment, realizing the man might be talking about someone other than Kunta.

"Someone else has been shot?" he asks.

"Yeah — my friend, they shot my friend!"

"How do you know this?"

"He just called me on the telephone, man!"

It's starting to seem that there may be indeed be a second victim somewhere. First came the dispatcher's call to Engine 14 wondering about the victim's wounds, as if she's gotten multiple calls for a shooting and is trying to determine if there is more than one incident that requires emergency attention. Now this man is telling the cops that his friend has been shot on a street one block over. While the police and dispatch try to sort it out, the firefighters focus their energy on Kunta. He is breathing quickly now and his chest is heaving sporadically.

"Keep breathing, keep breathing," Elmer says, cradling his head between her hands.

"Kunta, slow your breathing down," Penn says. "In through your nose, out through your mouth. In through your nose, out through your mouth. Come on, concentrate with me."

Elmer: "Slow it down, slow it down. There you go, that's good."

"Are you hurting anywhere else?" Penn asks. "Kunta? Listen to me. Do you think you got shot anywhere else other than where I'm holding the bandage?"

A mumble.

"Did you say your leg?"

A nod.

Elmer: "His leg."

As Schultz and Modahl begin searching his jeans for blood, Kunta begins to moan again: "Help me."

"We're helping ya, we're helping ya. Stay with us," Elmer reassures.

"Watch the ambulance, guys!" a cop yells from down the alley.

Penn looks up but doesn't see one. "Are they back there?"

"We've got an ambulance for you," Elmer tells Kunta. "They're coming."

The cop motions with his hand that the ambulance is going around the block to the other end of the alley.

"All right, thanks." Penn says.

It's now ten minutes to five. It's been nine minutes since the shooting call first came in at Station 14, and the dispatcher's voice blares out over Penn's radio.

"Ladder 10, a shooting, 2642 Fremont," the dispatcher intones. A second shooting victim a few blocks away has been confirmed.

"We've got some blood here, too, Cherie," Modahl says, pointing to a dark, wet spot inside of one of the man's pantlegs.

"Okay, cut 'em off of him." Penn says.

"Give me the scissors," Modahl says to Schultz, who already had them out. Modahl snips the denim from the ankle up to the knee.

"He's shot in the leg, we've got more blood," Penn says.

Elmer continues talking to the man, trying to keep him focused on his breathing, but he is clearly flagging. The ambulance has been backed up the alley, and Penn fills the paramedics in.

"Can't...breathe," Kunta groans.

"Stay with us, okay?"

Penn: "Help them with the stretcher." Schultz jumps up.

"Kunta, what we're getting ready to do is we're going to lift you into the ambulance, all right?" Penn says. "And get you out of this cold weather. Concentrate on your breathing — can you hear me? Kunta?...Do you get a pulse?"

The man who gave the firefighters Kunta's name is still standing nearby, a look of worry smeared across his face.

"Talk, K!" he shouts. "C'mon, man. Talk! Talk, K!"

Schultz and one of the paramedics have the stretcher ready.

"Pick him up," Penn orders. "Pick him up under his arms and let's get him on the cart. Here, get his shirt off."

Modahl cuts Kunta's shirt away.

"Kunta, raise your head up for us a little bit. One, two, three, go!"

Kunta is hoisted onto the stretcher and wheeled into the back of the ambulance. Schultz and Elmer climb in after him to assist the paramedics. Illuminated now by the better light of the ambulance, one of the paramedics spots an unusual lump in the middle of Kunta's chest. He investigates it with his fingers, and it turns out to be one of the bullets. It's trapped between Kunta's skin and sternum.

"We might have a second shooting victim a block over," Penn tells one of the paramedics as Ladder 10 goes wailing by, its flashing red lights visible between the houses to the east.

As the ambulance disappears around the corner, Kunta's blood-soaked shirt and jacket lie in a sticky heap on the ground.

A few blocks away, Rogalski has Anderson pull the ladder truck to a stop. A cop on the corner is waving to them, and Rogalski steps down from the cab. The lone officer informs him that witnesses just told him a man who had been shot in the stomach has

192

been whisked away in a vehicle. With no victim and no information on his current whereabouts, Rogalski ponders what to do next.

The ambulance bearing Kunta is now speeding off to the north with Schultz and Elmer still inside. Penn and Modahl are walking back toward Engine 14 with their medical bags, when a light-colored SUV comes tearing around the corner and heads into the alley. The vehicle screeches to a halt and the doors open. Penn and Modahl hear the police shouting, so they step behind a nearby garage for shelter. Penn is certain she's about to hear gunshots.

Instead, the SUV backs itself out of the alley and speeds away. Penn and Modahl step back into the alley and see the police waving them to come back in their direction. They jog over. Two houses south of where Kunta was lying, they find another man on his back, shot and bleeding from the stomach. Someone in the SUV shoved him out onto the pavement before it took off.

This second victim's location is relayed to Ladder 10, and Rogalski has his crew of Anderson, Drew, and Wright on the scene a few moments later. They find Penn and Modahl crouched over the man and the police sealing off the alley with thick rolls of bright yellow tape. The man looks to be about Kunta's age. He's wearing a Fat Albert T-shirt, and Modahl and Penn have already slashed his black jean legs open to check for wounds.

"What have you got?" Rogalski asks.

"He's doing fine, but he's cold," Penn says.

Anderson wheels around and heads back toward the truck to grab a blanket for the man. Rogalski stands by and allows Penn to continue with her command of the scene as Wright and Drew move in to help. They ready the oxygen.

"We're going to try to get some O-two on you to help you breathe, all right?" Penn says to the man. "And we're going to try to get some better light so we can see that you haven't been shot anywhere else, all right?"

She asks his name. Eric, he says.

"Hang in there, Eric."

Penn asks him some more questions about his medical history, but he is trembling so badly from the cold and trauma that his responses are difficult to discern.

"Eric, concentrate on your breathing, all right? You're not hit anywhere else but on your stomach," Penn says in an assuring tone.

The firefighters roll him gently on to his side to search for an exit wound but do not see one.

"Eric, was it a large-caliber gun, or was it a small one that hit you?" Rogalski asks.

"I don't know," he mutters. "Before I saw it, he shot."

A woman standing about fifty feet away in the alley is screaming at some of the other people standing around. She is short and stocky and full of rage.

"This has gotta stop!" she shrieks. "This is my community! This is my community! I have little kids that just came in this house a few minutes ago! They out here every day! They coulda been the ones that was shot!"

She continues to rant as the firefighters work. Penn hands Eric off to Rogalski's crew so she can go pick up Schultz and Elmer at the hospital. Before she and Modahl head out, Penn passes on what info she has gotten out of Eric to a paramedic that has arrived.

"He's very alert," Penn finishes.

"This one and the other one related at all?" the paramedic asks.

"I don't know, have to ask MPD, right here," she motions to one of the cops.

"Are you guys ready to come down the alley?" the officer asks the paramedic, referring to the ambulance. "We figured it was a crime scene, and he wasn't going to go through it for you, so he's driving around the block."

"All right. And yes, the shootings are related," the cop continues.

"Good guy, bad guy, same side?" the paramedic asks.

"Looks like they were both in the car together when they got shot. One guy ran and the other guy..."

A police sergeant walking by orders into his radio: "I need cops on foot in this alley, and I need this whole alley roped off."

Rogalski has Drew take Eric's vitals down while Wright continues speaking to him.

"How are you feeling now, Eric?"

"Get that blanket on him," Anderson says, and Eric is soon covered in a warming mantle of red wool.

Another paramedic arrives at the scene pushing a stretcher from the ambulance parked at the mouth of the alley.

"We've got the stretcher and we're getting ready to put you on the stretcher, all right?" Wright says. "Just relax though. We'll have you warm in a minute."

"Eric, keep your eyes open, okay?" Rogalski says.

Wright: "We're going to lift you up on here, okay? Don't do nothing, we've got you."

Paramedic: "On your count, you've got his head."

Wright: "One, two, three." Eric is up on the stretcher and the paramedics whisk him off to the ambulance.

The police are talking to witnesses and still trying to piece together what exactly happened — whether one or both of the men were in a vehicle when they were shot, whether they were shot at the same time, or by the same person, why the second victim had been dumped from the SUV. Someone says they think it was a drive-by.

"There's a white Caddy, a '96 white Caddy that's unaccounted for," an officer tells the sergeant in charge of the scene.

It's clear that, while the firefighters are finished here, the police have plenty of work ahead of them trying to figure out what happened. One officer walks a police dog into the alley. Both of them are wearing bulletproof vests. Cops are everywhere. The sergeant announces into his radio that he's got enough officers here for now, and that some of them are chasing a possible suspect.

Rogalski posts Drew in the ambulance to help the paramedics on their way to the hospital.

The rest of the ladder crew makes its way back to the rig. Wright is in the till tonight, and as he makes his way toward the back of the truck, a television cameraman steps into his path.

"Can you tell me what happened?" he asks.

Rank-and-file firefighters are not to speak to the media about emergency scenes. That's a job for the chiefs, so Wright simply smiles politely and shakes his head no, then pulls himself up into the till. After a trip over to North Memorial Medical Center to pick up their comrades, both Engine 14 and Ladder 10 roll back to the station.

It's a little after six now, and someone slides a large pan of lasagna for the evening clutch into the oven. By seven, the table has been set and the lasagna is bubbling and gooey as the firefighters dig in. They have not been eating for twenty seconds when the bell rings. A fire. Both rigs go. The nibbled lasagna begins to cool and coagulate even before the garage doors swing shut in the fire engines' wake.

Both rigs head west to Penn Avenue, then turn towards the north. The fire engines' lights are easily seen by the motorists on the wide, four-lane road, and most of them pull over to the side with plenty of time to spare in order to allow the rigs to get past. One vehicle, a green minivan, does not get out of the way as quickly. The driver seems to freeze and brings the van to a stop, at an angle, in the middle of the road. Modahl and Anderson slow the rigs down, then pass the minivan on both sides.

Arriving moments later at an apartment complex on Penn, a man in front says a car is burning in the back parking lot. Engine 14 accelerates around the corner and makes its way back down the alley. Rogalski has Anderson bring the ladder to a halt on the street in front, and the truckies proceed toward the back of the building on foot.

A small, four-door station wagon sits smoldering all by itself in the parking lot. No flame is showing, but the smoke is thick and seems to be gushing from every crevice in the vehicle. Penn does a quick walk-around of the car, then shouts, "Lay it!"

Elmer and Schultz snap into action and pull the inch-and-three-quarter line from the bed of the engine as Modahl revs up the pump. Anderson moves toward the front of the car and, with a few whacks of his axe, has the hood open in a matter of seconds. Wright opens the front passenger door a few inches, then slams it back shut when several long tongues of flame and a small mushroom cloud of smoke lunge out at him.

Elmer positions herself with the hose on the passenger's side of the car and Modahl charges the line. Elmer is facing into the wind as she waits to open the nozzle, so Rogalski suggests to the rookie that she move to the driver's side of the car before making her first attack. That way she won't get a wind-driven blast of smoke in her face as she works.

Elmer shifts her position. When Penn sees she's ready, she pulls open the rear door. The flames burst forth, but Elmer quickly takes them off their feet with a steady blast from the nozzle. At the exact same moment, Rogalski busts the front window out and is hit with a plume of black smoke. The fire is confined to the passenger compartment, and Elmer rotates back and forth to both sides of the car to finish it off.

There is little else for Rogalski and the ladder crew to do, so they pack up and head back toward the station. As Anderson eases the rig back into traffic, Rogalski twists around toward the back seat and tosses Drew an easy question.

"What do you think, Drew? The passenger compartment's filled with flame, but there's no flame in the engine compartment. Do you think we'll need the arson investigator for this one?"

The rookie just smiles and nods.

"Yeah," Rogalski sighs, turning back toward the front. "I think we'll need the arson investigator for this one."

Back at the station, the truckies reheat their lasagna and are just finishing it off when the engine crew returns. But before they can even sit back down, the engine is called out again on a fire run. Elmer sprints to the rig from the kitchen, leaving the microwave door open, her chilled lasagna sitting inside.

Engine 14 arrives at a house on Queen and finds a number of teenagers preparing for a party. An artificial smoke machine in the basement that they were intending to use later in the night had been activated, and someone called 911 when they saw the cottony white smoke filling the lower floor of the house. The teens are arguing over who is to blame as the firefighters mount up to head home.

Back at the station, the engine crew finally gets a break to finish its meal.

"Now I'm ready to eat," observes Schultz as he sits down to his microwaved pasta. "Before I wasn't hungry. Now I'm hungry."

An hour or so later, most everyone is in front of the station's various TV sets. The firefighters in the main TV room are watching a football game, when suddenly Penn's voice rings out across the apparatus floor.

"Hey, one of the guys from the shootings died!" She and Wright just saw it on the early news. There was a double shooting in North Minneapolis tonight, the reporter said, and one of the victims died in surgery at North Memorial. The firefighters debate which of the shooting victims seemed to be in worse shape, and it's a consensus — the first victim, Kunta. He seemed to have lost much more blood, and he had been hit twice in the torso. They'll probably have to wait to read about it in the newspaper to know for sure, but the bottom line is that someone they tried to save didn't make it.

Elmer sums it up: "That sucks."

After a short pause, Rogalski breaks the silence.

"I wonder if it's gang-related," he says.

"That's what I was wondering," Wright says. "If it was, that means we'll probably be busy tonight. Once they start hearing that so-and-so died, they'll be out."

Sure enough, a call comes in for another shooting less than 20 minutes later. As Engine 14 races back into what is becoming a bloody night, Wright wonders aloud whether a gang war's starting.

Engine 14 arrives at a house on Fremont, but the scene is much more calm and controlled than the earlier shootings. The paramedics are already there and helping a man to the ambulance. The man is walking under his own power and clutching a bandaged arm. The paramedics wave the firefighters off. As they move out, a lone man dressed all in black and wearing a black stocking cap watches from a nearby street corner. The tiny orange glow of a cigarette illuminates his face slightly. He gazes warily at the fire engine before turning around and disappearing into the night.

The remaining couple of hours leading up to midnight pass

quietly, mercifully. The only excitement comes when the crews see TV footage from the double shooting on the late news. Rogalski and Wright were caught on camera as they were moving around the rear of the ambulance.

"Hey Tom, look, we're stars," Wright says, a broad smile on his face.

Both crews are called out almost simultaneously in the early-morning hours — Engine 14 to a car accident, Ladder 10 with police to check out a fire alarm on Broadway. There is little work for the engine at what turns out to be a small fender-bender, while the ladder crew secures the building on Broadway. There is no fire. Police tell the crew that a woman said a man was attacking her so she pulled the fire alarm, but Rogalski has his crew check the building, just to be sure.

On their way back to the station, both crews notice how many police cars are patrolling the otherwise empty streets tonight.

As the other firefighters trundle back to bed shortly after one in the morning, Schultz pulls some leftover chicken from the refrigerator and pops it into the microwave, hoping it will help him get back to sleep.

The rest of the night passes without any more shootings, and Engine 14 is called out just once more to help a girl who is having trouble breathing. It's a little before eight in the morning now, and the B shift is arriving one at a time to relieve members of the A shift, many of whom are sitting around the tables in the dining room. Rogalski and Modahl are reading the paper, Anderson is watching TV, and Penn has nodded off, her head — a black MFD stocking cap pulled tightly over her scalp — resting on her arm. Loud whistles reverberate off the walls in the apparatus floor as the fresh crews test their SCBA gear in preparation for their shift.

Caouette, who spent the shift just past working at Station 15, shows up to get the scoop on all the action from last night. She heard all of the transmissions during the shootings come over the radio at the other station. The others fill her in on the details as they sip freshly brewed cups of strong firehouse coffee.

"And Heidi had her first one," Anderson concludes, referring to the rookie's first death on the job.

"How's she doing?" Caouette asks.

"She was kind of torn up about it," Anderson replies after a moment's pause.

"Really?"

Another pause.

"Yeah," Anderson continues. "I hope she knows it's just her first of many."

Epilogue

"You guys got your stuff all packed?" Rogalski asks Modahl and Anderson.

It's just before six o'clock in the morning, still dark, on New Year's Eve and the trio is riding back to the station in the cab of Ladder 10 following a fire run that turned out to be nothing more than an unusual odor coming from someone's furnace. Ladder 10 and Engines 14 and 20 sped from their beds to check it out, and the residents of the house on Fremont got a free, pre-dawn furnace inspection, complete with lights and sirens, compliments of the city of Minneapolis.

"Almost," Anderson replies.

"Getting there," Modahl says.

When their shift ends a little over two hours from now, the firefighters on the A shift of Engine 14 and Ladder 10 will say their goodbyes. In Minneapolis, the fire department holds an annual, seniority-based "re-draw" every fall to determine where everyone will be stationed for the upcoming calendar year. Penn and the rookies, Elmer and Drew, will remain on the A shift at Station 14. Schultz will also call Station 14 home for at least one more year, only he's going to the B shift. But the other A shift regulars are all moving on — Rogalski and Modahl to Rescue 1, Anderson to Ladder 4, Wright to Engine 17, Caouette to Engine 11, Wells to Engine 7. Some firefighters like the annual re-draw because it gives them a chance to work in a variety of stations during their career, and it allows the more veteran members of the department to work their way out to the slower stations as their careers wind down. But others feel it makes it tough for firefighters to build a strong a sense of camaraderie and pride in your company when you're always moving around. They would prefer a re-draw every couple years or so instead, but this is the way things are set up between the department and the union, so everyone makes the best of it.

After a final hour of uninterrupted sleep back at the station, those who are headed elsewhere begin pulling the last of their belongings from their lockers into boxes. They will take everything home with them before moving into their new quarters next shift. Wright and Caouette are both on vacation today, so they've already cleared out their stuff. Among the final items to come down from the lockers of Rogalski, Anderson, and Modahl are the photographs of their wives and children. All three have two kids age six or younger, and their smiling, cherubic likenesses are well represented on and inside their fathers' lockers.

Rogalski has several photos of his two young boys plastered to the gray door of a cabinet in his captain's office, including one of himself playing with one of his sons on a white, sandy beach somewhere. Anderson has pictures of his two daughters inside his locker, and a Winnie the Pooh coloring book page held to the outside by a "Three Stooges" magnet. The crayon scribbles applied by his daughters found their way well outside the lines of Tigger's body, but to the hulking firefighter it is a masterpiece worthy of public display. Two photos of Modahl's daughters, including one of them kneeling proudly in her soccer uniform, adorn the outside of their father's door.

For all firefighters, the photos of children, wives, husbands, boyfriends, girlfriends, and other loved ones serve as daily reminders of why they work so hard and, in many cases, who they're working to protect. On Halloween night a few years back, when arriving on the scene of an auto accident with Engine 10, then-rookie Modahl thought one of the vehicles involved look a lot like one of his own. After hopping from the rig and moving in closer, he quickly realized that it was indeed the vehicle his wife drove regularly. At the same moment, he heard a paramedic ask if there was a firefighter named Modahl here, and Shawn quickly rushed over to the ambulance, where he found his wife and one of his daughters being tended to. His daughter Haley, who was not yet three, had wanted to show off her costume — she was dressed as Dorothy from "The Wizard of Oz" — to her dad down at the fire station before going trick-or-treating, and Modahl's wife, Julie, was driving her there when the accident occurred.

Haley began crying when she saw her father. She had a cut on her head, and the blood had run down and spoiled her costume. Moments before, she had been so excited to show it to her daddy, and now the pretty dress had been ruined by the blood.

"Oh, Daddy, look at me," she sobbed in her disappointment. Modahl's heart broke for his little girl, but he was joyously relieved that neither she nor his wife were too badly injured.

With most of their things finally bagged up and dropped in their waiting vehicles, the firefighters chat and laugh with each other and the B-shifters coming on to relieve them. Today will be the last day at Station 14 for many on the B shift, too, and they're expecting a wild one, especially tonight. It almost always is on New Year's Eve.

Statistically, the week between Christmas and the turning of the year is a period of high fire incidence. It's hard to say why, but it probably has something to do with the general lethargy that can sweep over people this time of year, which can be a bad thing when half-melted candles, space heaters, and fireplaces are being used much of the time. Christmas trees stand brittle and dry as dust in people's living rooms, little more than tinsel-covered heaps of kindling by this point in the season. One spark from the fireplace or any other source can ignite a crackling, out-of-control blaze in no time.

"One of the saddest things you can see on this job is a Christmas tree fire," Rogalski says.

But fire is streaky. It often comes in bunches all around the city, while other times things can slow to a crawl. It's just the way it is. Things have been slow lately at Station 14, and the last two days for the A shift were particularly uneventful. The only real excitement came on the second-to-last shift of the year when a woman who had apparently been drinking blew through a stop sign on Lowry and T-boned an unsuspecting minivan just before one in the morning. The woman's car was spun around by the impact and she tried to flee in the opposite direction, but her vehicle's motor was too badly damaged to get her very far — only about a hundred feet away before it died.

Engine 14 found her outside her vehicle, lying on the grass between the street and the sidewalk. As they tried to discern her injuries, the police asked if she'd been drinking. She said no, but she never opened her eyes and her speech was badly slurred. The police also found a cool, wet beer can lying near her feet. As the firefighters and paramedics attempted to place a neck brace on the woman, who claimed to be experiencing back pain, she became violent and began thrashing her arms and moaning and shrieking wildly. They finally restrained her, strapped her to a backboard, and placed her into the ambulance.

A few other medical runs came through these last two days, along with a smattering of fire runs, none of which turned out to be workers. Part of the reason for the suddenly infrequent occurrence of fire throughout the city might be the unseasonably warm weather. The past few winters have been mild in Minnesota, relatively speaking, and this one has started out similarly temperate — very little snow, a spitting of ice, and temperatures that do little more than probe with one small toe beyond the freezing point on the thermometer. But it's still early, and the snow will come sometime soon, no doubt. And the temperatures will plummet, and the winds will pick up. The firefighters know it's bound to happen, and with it will come slick roads that make responding difficult, frozen hydrants and hose connections, and the rapid freezing of water as it is poured onto blazes fought in subzero temperatures. Burning structures with a good deal of flame showing are often attacked with water inside and outside, and water directed on the exteriors freezes fast in typical Minnesota winter conditions. The structure, if it's still standing after the fire is out, is often coated with dazzlingly beautiful ice shell and icicles. Firefighters call them "ice-castle fires." But while impressive, they are also dangerous, as the area around the structure becomes treacherous for gear-laden and fatigued firefighters, and the streets upon which the fire engines operated often have to be heavily sanded and salted by city trucks once the scene is clear.

Winter also means other dangers for Minneapolis firefighters, and the captains at Station 14 have been deliberate in their attempts to remind their troops, particularly the rookies, of the perils that will again rear their heads once the snow flies. For instance, the fire department is responsible for water rescues on the Mississippi River where it traverses the city. Water rescues are always tricky in any weather, thanks to the various bridges, falls, and other manmade structures that play tricks with the water current at various points along the river. Frozen surfaces and freezing water beneath make things even more treacherous, a point Rogalski hammered home to Elmer as they gazed out over the river from one of the department's boat-launch points yesterday morning. Rogalski has been part of a number of ice rescues since he joined the department, two of which ended up in living color on the pages of the Star Tribune. The first was in December 1994. A man jumped from the Third Avenue Bridge and into the ice-choked Mississippi. A fire department boat crew was closing in on the man when he slipped over St. Anthony Falls and was out of their reach. The man was soon within about 30 feet of the east river bank, and Rogalski, wearing a reddish, cold-weather "Gumby" suit, stepped into the river and swam out between floating ice chunks to rescue the man, who was still alive and was whisked to the hospital. Rogalski not only received commendation from the department and a good dose of media coverage for his heroics, he was further rewarded about two years later when the man he saved called to thank him for giving him a second chance at life.

Not every ice rescue has such a fortunate ending, however. In the other rescue in which Rogalski was involved that made the paper — this one in 1998 — a 12-year-old boy fell through the icy crust on Powderhorn Lake. Rogalski and fellow firefighter Julie Stepan found the boy and pulled him up from about a dozen feet of water, but he was already dead.

Rogalski also recently made a point of urging the rookies to be extremely wary when they are called out to assist with accidents on the city's extensive freeway system. It's up to the fire department's drivers to park the rigs so they shield the scene of the accident from high-speed traffic, but that does not always neutralize the danger, and icy roads and diminished visibility create increasingly perilous conditions for highway operations. Indeed, the last firefighter the department lost in the line of duty was Leroy Swenson, who was killed in 1997 when a truck fell on top of him during a response on an icy freeway. Swenson was a thirty-one-year veteran of the department who was nearing retirement and looking forward to spending a lot of his time at his cabin on Lake Superior. Rogalski related the terrible story to the rookies, who took it in with appropriate solemnity, nodding slowly and attentively, Elmer's face curling into a silent grimace as Rogalski related the grave details of the accident. She and Drew had been on the job for a little more than a month and were clearly settling in well with their coworkers and responsibilities on emergency scenes. The captains wanted to make sure they were always on their toes, never sliding into a complacency that could get them hurt, or worse. When she became a captain, a superior had told Penn that her main job — her absolute paramount priority — was to make sure that her entire crew was still standing at the end of each year. Rogalski, Penn, Kris Lemon, Tim Baynard, and the other captains who sat in charge of Ladder 10 and Engine 14 on the A shift steered their firefighters safely through another hectic year on the North Side.

And once again Engine 14 and Ladder 10 had been called on to do it all — to extinguish house fires, garage fires, car fires, garbage fires; to treat victims of shootings, multiple shootings, stabbings, domestic assaults, and car crashes; to deliver babies; to calm and treat people suffering from drug overdoses, epileptic seizures, or other forms of delirium that put both the patient and firefighters in harm's way. The companies responded to 3,816 calls for help in all in twelve months. When things went bad in their part of the city, they were always there to help clean up the mess.

Following the A shift's final evening meal together, Penn called all six of the firefighters on duty together to meet one last time with her and Rogalski. They gathered on the apparatus floor near the rear of the station, where Penn thanked everyone for the service they provided the city of Minneapolis over the past year. She acknowledged that the station had dealt with a lot during the past twelve months, both within the station and without, and that she and the other captains were grateful everyone stayed focused and worked hard when the time came.

"When that bell rang, we put everything else aside and came together as a team," Penn said as she sat on a chair near the rear of Ladder 10, Rogalski leaning against the big rig and nodding his agreement. "When that bell rang, we went to work, and we got the job done."

About the author

Brett Knapp (also known as "Scoop," particularly to ladder truck captains who can't remember his name) is an award-winning freelance writer who has lived in the Twin Cities since 1992. Two of his relatives are retired firefighters, and he was often the first to call dibs on the nozzle when it came time for the kids' games at local fire department picnics. This is his first book.